THE EVERYTHING®

LOVE SIGNS BOOK
2ND EDITION

Dear Reader,

I recently found this quote from the illustrious financial wizard J. P. Morgan: "Millionaires don't use astrology. Billionaires do." Hah! I thought. Funny . . . and true! We've used the planets and the stars as our guide since the fourth century B.C. Why? Because they influence everything we do in life—from health to luck to love. Just ask Johannes Kepler, Isaac Newton, or Louis Pasteur.

I'm always surprised when people ask me if astrology is real. Predictably, their skepticism has to do with an aversion to the generalizations that have plagued astrology since the beginning: Virgo is finicky; Leo is arrogant; Sagittarius has wanderlust. Where is the three-dimensional person? Where is the beauty of the individual? In truth, claims such as these are stereotypical, at best, and inaccurate, at worst.

I'm from New York, but I lived in Italy for many years—and in Mexico, before that. People sigh when I tell them about my time in Tuscany and my real fairy-tale life. I say: Anyone can have what I have. You just have to know where to look. Here.

Read up and find out. Your future awaits.
Warm wishes,

Jenni Kosarin

The EVERYTHING Series

These handy, accessible books give you all you need to tackle a difficult project, gain a new hobby, or even brush up on something you learned back in school but have since forgotten. You can read from cover to cover or just pick out information from our four useful boxes.

 Alerts: Urgent warnings

 Essentials: Quick handy tips

 Facts: Important snippets of information

 Questions: Answers to common questions

When you're done reading, you can finally say you know **EVERYTHING®**!

PUBLISHER Karen Cooper

DIRECTOR OF ACQUISITIONS AND INNOVATION Paula Munier

MANAGING EDITOR, EVERYTHING® SERIES Lisa Laing

COPY CHIEF Casey Ebert

ASSISTANT PRODUCTION EDITOR Melanie Cordova

ACQUISITIONS EDITOR Lisa Laing

ASSOCIATE DEVELOPMENT EDITOR Hillary Thompson

EDITORIAL ASSISTANT Ross Weisman

EVERYTHING® SERIES COVER DESIGNER Erin Alexander

LAYOUT DESIGNERS Erin Dawson, Michelle Roy Kelly, Elisabeth Lariviere, Denise Wallace

Visit the entire Everything® series at *www.everything.com*

THE
EVERYTHING®

Love
SIGNS
BOOK

2ND EDITION

Use astrology to find your perfect partner!

Jenni Kosarin

Aadamsmedia

Avon, Massachusetts

Copyright © 2012, 2004 by F+W Media, Inc.
All rights reserved.
This book, or parts thereof, may not be reproduced in any
form without permission from the publisher; exceptions are
made for brief excerpts used in published reviews.

An Everything® Series Book.
Everything® and everything.com® are registered trademarks
of F+W Media, Inc.

Published by
Adams Media, a division of F+W Media, Inc.
57 Littlefield Street, Avon, MA 02322. U.S.A.
www.adamsmedia.com

ISBN 10: 1-4405-2819-5
ISBN 13: 978-1-4405-2819-4
eISBN 10: 1-4405-2914-0
eISBN 13: 978-1-4405-2914-6

Printed in the United States of America.

10   9   8   7   6   5   4   3   2   1

Library of Congress Cataloging-in-Publication Data
is available from the publisher.

This publication is designed to provide accurate and authoritative information with regard to the subject matter covered. It is sold with the understanding that the publisher is not engaged in rendering legal, accounting, or other professional advice. If legal advice or other expert assistance is required, the services of a competent professional person should be sought.
—From a *Declaration of Principles* jointly adopted by a Committee of the American Bar Association and a Committee of Publishers and Associations

Many of the designations used by manufacturers and sellers to distinguish their product are claimed as trademarks. Where those designations appear in this book and Adams Media was aware of a trademark claim, the designations have been printed with initial capital letters.

This book is available at quantity discounts for bulk purchases.
For information, please call 1-800-289-0963.

ACKNOWLEDGMENTS

Love to Paul and Donna Kosarin (Sagittarius and Pisces, respectively) . . . superb editors—you two missed your calling. Your genuine and generous affection for one another—continually romantic after fifty-two (plus) years—sets the bar for all potential soul mates. You have inspired me and everyone around you with the true love you have. Thank you for everything you are, everything you represent, and everything you've done.

My warm thanks also go to (Virgo) acquisitions editor Bethany Brown for her constant guidance in the past—and to Laura Daly (Leo), too, for going that extra distance. I'd also like to thank Hillary Thompson (Sagittarius) . . . And an extra-BIG thank-you goes to Lisa Laing (Sagittarius) for her extraordinary support: I've appreciated every bit of it.

Thank you all!

Contents

The Top 10 Love Sign Couples

1. Pisces woman/Sagittarius man: Who says Fire and Water clash? This couple sizzles!

2. Cancer woman/Leo man: Rocket launchers and firecrackers. You can't beat these two if they form a deep bond of trust.

3. Gemini woman/Gemini man: Both like to be playful and silly; if they play fair, it can work.

4. Scorpio woman/Leo man: These two go together so well that it's a little scary. Neither back down—and that's good.

5. Libra woman/Capricorn man: Libra brings out Capricorn's happy, calm side: If he can remain nonconfrontational, he can bring some security to her life.

6. Cancer woman/Scorpio man: If she can overlook his political views and deal with the stress that comes from his work, they're a match made in heaven.

7. Aquarius woman/Taurus man: Taurus is sensuous and daring; she's intrigued by his down-to-earth approach to life.

8. Scorpio woman/Sagittarius man: Thank goodness Sag is a real man, she thinks. She also loves the fact that people look up to him.

9. Libra woman/Libra man: Who would've thought? Somehow, though, they truly balance each other out.

10. Scorpio woman/Taurus man: You won't find a stranger couple—they're odd together, but it seems to work . . . especially if he lets her lead.

Introduction

> *"Courteous reader, Astrology is one of the most ancient sciences, held in high esteem of old, by the Wise and the Great. Formerly, no Prince would make war or peace; nor any General fight in battle. In short, no important affair was undertaken without first consulting an Astrologer."*
>
> —Benjamin Franklin (1706–1790),
> signer of the Declaration of Independence,
> scientist, printer, economist, philosopher

Heartbreak. A love gone wrong. A whirlwind romance and then a big breakup. These sound like the basic themes of your typical bad country song. (They may well be.) But they're also moments justifiably crooned about—unfortunate, albeit necessary parts of life. And they happen without warning, without reason . . . and sometimes, as luck would have it, without an essential never-ending stock of double-fudge chocolate chunk ice cream.

Really, love sometimes feels like an affliction that's forced on you in an instant, without your control: Achoo! And then it's gone as quickly as it came.

Now, what if someone could clue you in to the mysteries and secrets of your "other half" before you became irrevocably involved? What if someone could give you sound advice before the bedlam and the bother, the inevitable heartache? Even better, what if you could know exactly what you're looking for in a perfect mate and know who could be right or wrong for you even before the first date? It sounds impossible, doesn't it?

It's not; it's real. It's called love astrology. And you could learn it all from this comprehensive book—the key to discovering your future before it happens. From the information gathered here, you'll get a glimpse of the future, what to expect from a potential life partner, and what an astrological soul mate really is. You'll understand your other half's likes and dislikes on all fronts: financial, emotional, spiritual, intellectual, and sexual. In other words, you'll discover everything essential for personally assessing the true possibilities of your future together.

Above all, you should always remember that nothing is set in stone. There are always ways to overcome obstacles and handicaps. If you find the man or woman of your dreams, don't rule that person out! Instead, read everything there is to know about him or her here. Then go about making future plans accordingly. Love signs astrology exists to help, not hinder, you. Arm yourself before the battle, and you'll always come out ahead.

In short, life is complex; people are complex. Astrology is not. It can be learned. Sun-sign matches are one way to predict love compatibility—but they're not enough. Your Venus, for example, is your love sign—a spiritual beacon, how you react in love. A compatible sign in Mercury indicates a meeting of the minds. This one book brings all these themes together with easy-to-read charts in the back—all accessible with a birth date and an interest.

There are also essential (fun! naughty!) sexual tips that will work before and during intimacy, and seduction techniques based on astrological clues.

In effect, love can be a scary subject . . . and so can handing your heart out on a silver platter. But love astrology is simple. If you absorb the necessary information here, one can easily be applied to the other. Because once you combine the two, you have the relationship advantage.

And that's nothing to sneeze at.

Love Signs
Compatibility Quiz

The following compatibility quiz is for fun—and it will also help you figure out some mysteries about yourself, your lover, or any other potential mates. One thing is for sure: It will uncover some pretty unexpected things! When you're finished, check the scoring at the end to see what this reveals about your love style and which signs may be the right ones for you . . . according to your answers. Always remember that free will exists and that astrology is meant to show you the signs with which you'll get along easiest (because of how their natures match up with yours). However, there are no definitive answers: There never are in love. Only *you* know what is in your heart . . . and you should follow it. Enjoy!

1. **You meet someone new—someone you really like. If your new love went digging into your past, what would you worry most about being discovered?**
    A. Childhood traumas
    B. Your true age
    C. Exes you're still in contact with
    D. Promiscuity and/or cheating

2. **After the best first date of your life, what would you do?**
    A. Dream in Technicolor and obsess relentlessly until the next time you meet.
    B. Tweet everyone and put photos up on Facebook. Why not?
    C. Tell only a close friend or family member and hope for the best. After all, who really knows what's going to happen?
    D. Go on a date with a new partner. You never put all your eggs in one basket.

3. **With the right person, you're a sucker for:**
    A. Sincere words of affection
    B. Flowers and dinner . . . or tickets to a football game
    C. Cuddling, holding hands, and kissing
    D. Stock options

4. **Your partner tells you a huge, juicy secret (about someone you both know) and asks you not to tell. What do you do?**
    A. Take it to the grave
    B. Blab to someone—you can't help it
    C. Tell your mother or sibling
    D. Tell only a couple of people who don't know your partner

5. **With your longest relationship, how were you together?**
    A. So alike—like mirror images of one other . . . a little scary
    B. Almost complete opposites—but you balanced each other out
    C. A reversal of typical gender roles
    D. It was love, but probably not the love of your life

6. **What was the quickest you ever fell in love?**
   A. One day—it was love at first sight
   B. After a few months
   C. A couple of months, and after there was real trust
   D. Pretty quickly—you felt it from the beginning but didn't know if you should trust it

7. **At your very worst, what do you do when you're stuck in traffic?**
   A. Crank up the tunes to blur out the chaos
   B. Look in the mirror or at people in other cars and try to distract yourself
   C. Mutter to yourself, your mood quickly going south
   D. Road rage—you yell at the guy in front of you and call him names even though you know he can't hear you

8. **What is the one thing you couldn't live without in a partner?**
   A. Charm and charisma
   B. Great looks
   C. Affection
   D. Financial security

9. **How superstitious are you?**
   A. Extremely superstitious. You've dabbled in everything: chanting spells, bathing in "magical herbs," wishing on stars . . . .
   B. A little. You may own something that brings you good luck (lucky cap/shirt or rabbit's foot), or you'll read your horoscope sometimes—and follow it.
   C. Definitely. The number 666 means something to you. You make a wish every day at 11:11 (or another time). You flip coins to make decisions.
   D. No way. You're not superstitious at all.

10. **What would you most likely do right before saying "I do"?**
    A. Obsess, mostly—and make sure neither one of you gets cold feet.
    B. Say, "I've got my things packed . . . Let's run off to Maui and elope."
    C. Make sure the in-laws and extended family don't get in the way too much.
    D. Get a prenup signed.

11. **After dating someone for a month, you accidentally find a box full of pornography DVDs. What do you do?**
    A. Laugh about it
    B. Suggest you watch one together
    C. Wait a few days, then casually mention pornography to see if your new love will bring it up without prodding
    D. Get a little horrified

12. **What type of mate turns you on?**
    A. A sweet, intellectual, funny, and romantic wise-ass
    B. A think-outside-of-the box kind of person
    C. A cerebral, spiritual soul who has traveled quite a bit
    D. A "tell it like it is" person . . . even if it hurts to hear the truth

13. **You're at a party. Your mate of two months is spending the entire night with an ex instead of you. What's the worst you're capable of doing?**
    A. Leaving without saying goodbye
    B. Confronting your mate in public and demanding not to be ignored
    C. Flirting with the most attractive person in the room
    D. Waiting until after you have left the party to have a private confrontation
    E. Doing way worse things than the others listed above

14. **Who would you be more likely to have casual sex with?**
    A. A good friend you've always been attracted to
    B. A sexy stranger you just can't resist
    C. An ex who broke up with you
    D. Someone from your past whom you have always fantasized about

15. **Pick one thing that would NOT define how you approach most situations. You're not likely to say _____:**
    A. I cannot.
    B. I will not.
    C. I do not.
    D. I should not.

16. **What do you do if your date is rude to a server?**
    A. Defend the server
    B. Make a joke about it to lighten the mood
    C. Lose respect for your date
    D. Tell your date to calm down

17. **When you see a person of the opposite sex for the first time, what "strikes" you?**
    A. A smile
    B. His style of dress
    C. How he walks
    D. The way he interacts with other people

18. **You're on a third date with a person you really like. Your date is flirting constantly and shamelessly with the young bartender. What will you do?**
    A. Decide to never see your date again
    B. Hope it's just a one-time thing

19. **After a heated argument, your mate of three months unexpectedly breaks up with you and leaves. What do you do?**
    A. Wait for him to contact you . . . Why risk getting hurt again?
    B. Call and yell or cry
    C. Suffer in silence but send a friendly e-mail with nothing about "the two of you"
    D. Text or get in contact another way . . . after a week (or maybe a month)

20. **How do you feel about major PDA (public displays of affection) between you and a partner?**
    A. You love it, but only when you're really in the mood.
    B. It's great; you live your life like no one's watching.
    C. It's necessary.
    D. Displays of affection should be private, NOT public.

21. **What do you do to get over a really bad day?**
    A. Watch a movie on TV that really makes you smile
    B. Nap a little, turn off the phone, grab a bottomless bowl of munchies, and shut out the world
    C. Find someone you've already been intimate with to have sex—or do some other pleasurable thing to lift your spirits
    D. Surf around on your computer, take a walk, or do things around the house to distract yourself

22. **Which type best describes you?**
    A. A lover: You're a true romantic.
    B. A free spirit: You're independent and like it that way.
    C. A giver: You sacrifice a lot for the ones you love.
    D. A doer. You love to do things for people you care about.

23. **What would you most likely do on a day off?**
    A. Have a good meal out
    B. Go to the movies

c. Dig into a really great book and/or do some tidying around the house

D. Take a day trip

24. What profession would your ideal match have?

A. A famous writer/artist/creative type

B. A well-off plastic surgeon or doctor

c. A renowned master, guru, yogi, teacher, or coach

D. An important CEO of a large company

E. A potential mate's profession doesn't matter to you

25. You fall in "like" too easily when someone:

A. Is clever with the gift of gab

B. Is physically attractive

c. Has incredible passion for things—for example, job, charities, music, etc.

D. Has money and likes to lavish it on you

26. What do you think is the best strategy for a blind date?

A. Talk on the phone first to feel things out before you go.

B. Just go. If you're not having fun, you can always say you have to get up early.

c. Correspond through a few e-mails before meeting.

D. Text or e-mail and then have coffee. That way you're not stuck with a bad date all night.

27. When faced with a difficult decision in life, you typically:

A. Ask everyone you know, then figure it out and decide

B. Don't think about it too much—you usually know the right thing to do

c. Always go with your gut or wait for the answer to hit you

D. Weigh all the risks and benefits by yourself, then decide

28. **Which of these could you never tolerate in a long-term relationship?**
    A. Constant restlessness and hyperactivity
    B. Antisocial behavior
    C. Someone who agrees with everything you say
    D. Someone who disagrees with everything you say

29. **After a serious heartbreak, how long does it take you to pick up the pieces and move on?**
    A. Two years, maybe. When you fall, you fall hard.
    B. You were on to the next one within six months (but you might still think about the first one).
    C. About a year, but the next one was better.
    D. There's no set time frame. But when you do find someone new, and you consider your past love, you wonder, "What was I thinking?"

30. **You're on a first date, and the chemistry is really intense. What are you thinking?**
    A. "Is this 'The One'?"
    B. "I wonder how we'd be in bed together."
    C. "When will we kiss?"
    D. "Everything is great. He must be hiding something."

31. **What characteristic about a potential mate might make you a little more intrigued, not less?**
    A. Abandonment issues
    B. Eccentricity
    C. A bit of compulsion about neatness or germs
    D. A sarcastic, biting sense of humor

32. **If someone you like pays you a compliment on your shoes, how do you respond?**
    A. You say thank you.
    B. You say thank you and make a joke about it.
    C. You say thank you and return the compliment.
    D. You say thank you and reveal where you bought the shoes.

33. **What makes you laugh?**
    A. Ironic, subtle, and clever situational humor
    B. Slapstick—people tripping over things
    C. Funny banter; good timing
    D. Teasing and strange, off-beat humor

34. **What would your family members say is your biggest flaw when it comes to you choosing a partner?**
    A. Too crazy
    B. Too needy
    C. Too immature
    D. Too difficult

35. **You see an obviously intoxicated thirty-year-old woman in the street, stumbling and looking confused. What would you do?**
    A. Pretend you don't see her.
    B. Avoid her. She's probably on drugs.
    C. Look around to see if someone else can help.
    D. Help her somehow.

Scoring

a = 1 point
b = 2 points
c = 3 points
d = 4 points
Question 13:
e = subtract 4 points
Question 18:
a = 10 points
b = 3 points

Question 24:
a = 10 points
b = 1 point
c = 10 points
d = 10 points
e = 10 points
Question 35:
a = subtract 3 points
b = subtract 10 points
c = 4 points
d = 15 points

Add up your points and find your sign below. Remember that this is just a short guide to the signs *you would most naturally* go best with (depending on the person in question with whom you're matching). Only the most recommended matches are starred with an asterisk before the sign.

Most Compatible Signs

Aries	
Score 35–85	*Aries, *(Cancer man), Scorpio, (Leo man)
Score 85–140	*Aries, (Aquarius man), Scorpio, *(Cancer man), Cancer woman, (Pisces woman), (Leo man)
Taurus	
Score 35–85	Gemini, Aquarius, *(Scorpio woman)
Score 85–140	*Scorpio, (Virgo woman), *Aquarius, *(Gemini woman)
Gemini	
Score 35–85	*Gemini, Aquarius, (Leo man), *Taurus
Score 85–140	*Gemini, *Taurus, Virgo, *(Virgo woman)
Cancer	
Score 35–85	*(Scorpio man), *(Leo man), Aries, (Pisces woman)
Score 85–140	*(Leo man), *(Scorpio man), Pisces
Leo	
Score 35–85	*Gemini, Sagittarius, *(Cancer woman), *(Scorpio woman), Leo
Score 85–140	Sagittarius, *Gemini, Aquarius, *(Scorpio woman), Cancer
Virgo	
Score 35–85	Gemini, *(Aquarius woman), Leo, Libra
Score 85–140	Capricorn, Libra, Gemini, Leo, *(Aquarius woman)

Libra	
Score 35–85	*Libra, Aquarius, Virgo, Scorpio
Score 85–140	*Libra, Pisces, Taurus, Aquarius
Scorpio	
Score 35–85	*Leo woman, Sagittarius, *Cancer woman, *Taurus, (Scorpio woman)
Score 85–140	Ditto above plus: Scorpio, Pisces, *Taurus
Sagittarius	
Score 35–85	(*Pisces woman), Cancer, *Scorpio
Score 85–140	(*Pisces woman), *Scorpio, Cancer, Pisces
Capricorn	
Score 35–85	*Aquarius, (Leo man), Cancer, Capricorn
Score 85–140	Libra, Taurus, Aquarius, *(Aquarius man), (Leo man), Capricorn
Aquarius	
Score 35–85	*Aquarius, Libra, Leo
Score 85–140	*Aquarius, Leo, Capricorn
Pisces	
Score 35–85	*Sagittarius, *Scorpio, Leo
Score 85–140	*Sagittarius, *Scorpio

You've just had a glimpse of some great recommendations for your sign, but that's not the end. There are many opportunities with *other* signs. Simply go through the chapters and read through. Please know that not all Scorpios (*every* one you meet) or another recommended sign, for example, are for you; it always depends on the particular person. Two people's chemistry is also significant—how you are *together*. And if a match is not recommended, remember, love knows no bounds. So go for it! Now . . . good luck to the two of you!

CHAPTER 1

Aries

Let's talk about the Ram. Powerful, charismatic, a real star, Aries is the first sign of the zodiac and quite a charmer, too, in love and romance. Some of the stereotypes associated with the Aries personality are true and some aren't. Let's have a look at a more three-dimensional Aries. Here, we put the pieces together and finally make sense of it all.

Can You Handle Aggressive Aries?

1. **What is one thing Aries "is" but can't handle in a mate?**
   A. Spontaneous
   B. Affectionate
   C. Judgmental
   D. Bossy

2. **What ability does Aries have above all other signs?**
   A. To start and finish projects
   B. To debate and argue something until the other backs down
   C. To be diplomatic, always
   D. To keep quiet if something is bothering him until the time is right

3. **True or False: Aries is considered the baby of the zodiac.**
   A. True
   B. False

4. **Name the phrase that would most turn Aries on?**
   A. Your place or mine?
   B. Over here . . . let's not get caught.
   C. Anytime, anywhere.
   D. I'm always ready for you.

5. **With an Aries lover who's not doing something exactly the way you like it, you must be:**
   A. Bold. Just say it.
   B. Quiet. Don't say anything.
   C. Jocular. Lighten up the mood.
   D. Sweet. Compliment, then say it.

6. **If Aries breaks up with you without a good reason, giving you a harsh "I never want to see you again," what should you do?**
   A. Leave Aries alone. If the Ram wants you, the Ram will find you.
   B. Call directly to talk.
   C. Send a really well-written e-mail.
   D. Text pictures from your phone to show you're having fun.

7. **Your new Aries mate wants to go out on the town and party, but doesn't invite you. You should:**
   A. Do the same thing with your friends
   B. Warn Aries not to cheat, dance with someone else, or take someone else's phone number
   C. Wait until your Aries man is out, then call a few times to check up
   D. Say "Have fun!", ask nothing, and go about your business

8. **In bed, Aries's style is usually:**
   A. Soft and sweet
   B. Dominant and naughty
   C. Passionate and romantic

9. **If you sleep with Aries on the first date, can it still lead to a long-term relationship?**
   A. Definitely—no problem.
   B. Most likely not—unless you knew each other from before.
   C. Most likely yes—especially if it was fun.
   D. How good was it? Really good? Then the answer is yes.

10. **What turns Aries off?**
    A. Someone who likes porn
    B. Someone who doesn't fight back
    C. Someone who gets too much attention from others
    D. Someone who's arrogant

Answers: 1. c, 2. b, 3. a, 4. b, 5. d, 6. a, 7. d, 8. b, 9. b, 10. b

The Aggressor

It's true. Aries is aggressive. But more specifically, Aries is a go-getter. In romance or business, Aries always aims to come out on top. He's instinctive and a great negotiator. His tactics can be a bit harsh, but he's charming, too, and usually gets what he wants (sometimes rubbing a few people the wrong way in the process, though). People gravitate toward him because he's never boring. Unfortunately, many Aries never quite get to the point where they're actually happy with their work. Somehow this always affects their love situations. In truth, it's never really about the money, though that's always a nice incentive. Instead, it has more to do with recognition and status; what success brings with that. Yes, work is very important to Aries—man or woman. And there's a very good reason for this.

Aries are the children of the zodiac. However mature an Aries is, he will want something not quite within his reach—not unlike a child who has had a rubber ducky taken from him in the bathtub. Unfortunately, this affects his way of dealing with romance. When he's not content with his work life, there is nothing a partner can do to make him happy. He can become moody and lose his enchanting sense of humor. When this happens, watch out!

The Perceptive Eye

There is one difference, though, from the other, less fixed signs: Aries can be practical about his options, intuitively sensing what he's good at. Therefore, Aries will attack a problem—whether in love or business—at full force but with a discerning eye. He does this because if he can't conquer and win, his ego will have a hard time of it. He can rush head-on into any romantic or business situation, but know this—Aries will eventually catch on and weigh the situation completely in definitive terms, good or bad. If it's the latter, he'll be out the door without a second glance.

❗ Alert

Aries will never methodically search out advice. When it comes to a tough situation, he'll take others' ideas and apply them to the situation at hand, calling them his own. But beware! If you call him on it, he may just get defensive and turn everything around on you.

At his best, Aries is romantic, exciting, and exceptionally fun to be with. Though he's more inclined to pounce on a grand romance and then pull back in an instant, he does make a loyal partner in the long run—in his own way. True, Aries is not the most faithful sign of the zodiac, though he expects you to be. But he does esteem and cherish any significant other with whom he's chosen to spend his life.

Seeking Perfection

Another thing not highly known about Aries men and women is that they're seriously idealistic. Though Aries is pragmatic with goals, he wants more than anything to achieve greatness. This, too, filters into home life. When it comes to love and family, Aries will look for his ideal partner—though chances are that he won't find her early in the game.

Strangely enough, Aries is the "least guilty" sign of the zodiac. In other words, like a child, Aries is always convinced of his innocence, believing that if he messes up (or cheats!), it's warranted—at least in his case. Don't bother reminding Aries you were right. He's already mentally reshaped events to accommodate his take of the situation.

Don't try fawning all over Aries, either, telling him he's fascinating. He knows it already, and he'll start to think, "That's right.
I am fascinating. In fact, I'm probably too good for you."

✓ Fact

A contradiction in terms, Aries wants an easy-going
partner—but also needs a good chase. A perfect love
match for Aries is someone who is neither high-mainte-
nance nor a pushover. This is a tricky blend but one that is
worthy of the typical Aries's affections.

Though family is very important to him, many Aries have
considerable difficulty with estranged brothers or sisters or critical parents. This is one of the reasons that he'll search for the
ultimate partner. Sometimes Aries even gets engaged not once
but two or three times. When he's signed the contract, though,
you'll most likely have won an Aries forever. It's not easy to
get him to the altar: The faster, the better, though . . . that's the
advice. Once accomplished, it's probably a union that will last.

A Power Play

If you've ever been involved with an Aries for a long period,
at some point you've no doubt come to a standstill in the relationship (around six months?). Aries is inexplicably drawn to
situations that require a bigger scheme. This means that her
undeniable wisdom will eventually enter into the picture. She
needs to feel useful and to apply her incredible wisdom to make
everything "right." Aries is probably convinced that her way
is the best way. If she's challenged too often, she'll give a few
telltale signs that she's had enough. Then she'll just walk away,

without warning. Though she may place the occasional ego call to determine whether the significant other is still interested, she doesn't necessarily care what the answer is either way. Once she's made up her mind, that's it. When this happens, it's a sure sign the relationship is over.

Question

Can a fling with an Aries turn into something more? Probably not. You'll have to start with good behavior from the very beginning. Aries rates her partners. She wants a perfect mate, not just a play buddy.

Aries likes to be in control of things—but she'll despise you if you can't stand up to her in a way she deems worthy of her respect. Call it power, or call it power play, Aries will not be manipulated to do another's bidding, though she'll still want her man to be strong. She'll also want someone who's calm and cool but who can effortlessly keep up with her adventures without stifling her. It's a tall order for an Aries woman, but one she requires to keep the boredom at bay.

"Give Me Freedom, Or . . ."

Power does have a key influence in the Aries relationship, though it affects this sign in a rather odd way. All Aries are independent and need a lot of space. Even though she loves affection, sincerity, and unconditional love from a partner she prizes, Aries still wants the freedom to go out or stay in when she feels like it. This is a very delicate balance to achieve. No one can hold an Aries down—and no one should. The one true way to maintain a person of this sign is to let her do what she wants to do. Give her space and freedom. If she's truly the one for you, she'll be back. Aries hates to be proved wrong: If she's invested time and money into any effort (including a relationship), she won't be so quick to watch it fizzle out before her eyes.

The Art of Attraction

It's stupid to play games in love, right? Wrong. Aries will almost never go for the easy target. For Aries, man or woman, the chase is essential and lends to the excitement. In fact, add a sense of "hope we don't get caught," and you've found yourself a winning plan. Granted, this will only work for the beginning period of the courtship. Read on to determine what will keep an Aries by your side.

The Long Haul

Sure, Aries seems jealous and possessive. He is, to a point—though not to the degree of Scorpio, Cancer, or even Sagittarius. Truthfully, Aries simply cannot imagine someone would actually leave him for another . . . and he's usually right. He's sexy and charming—macho, even. With Aries, jealousy is almost a test, as in, "Let's see how much my partner loves me." And with that answer, he'll be free to go back to more important tasks—typically related to career and work.

🌟 Essential

Aries wants a stable partner: one who's emotionally balanced and independent. Aries will also control the situation by seeking out security. If you're faithful and know how to stand up to Aries, you've got a mate for life.

Aries needs to know that you have your own life, your own friends, career, and outside interests. Aries distrusts clingers-on and doesn't want an overly jealous mate (though a tiny bit of jealousy, ironically, does help him feel secure). If you're out of work, don't stay that way for long. Aries won't tolerate it.

Here's another secret about the Ram—he's a social beast. If not for any other reason, Aries likes to be out there, ready to butt heads with others, ready to defend his cause. He needs to be noticed and recognized for something: his cool savvy, his sharp business sense, his charm, whatever. He's always on the lookout for contacts, whether professional or personal. Aries will also go in spurts, being social and then staying home for periods of time. If you want to keep Aries, let him do what he needs to do. Live your life, and make room for him in it. He'll push his way back in when he's ready.

The Little Stuff Counts

Like other Fire signs, Aries loves to be worshipped. Unlike Leo, who tends to be more modest about it, Aries puts it out there, letting you build up his ego as much as you can. After all, he deserves it, he believes. Insult Aries in a hard-nosed or vulgar way, and you'll be heading in the wrong direction. Present an issue to Aries delicately, on a politically correct platter, and you'll earn the respect of any Aries, male or female. The truth is, Aries actually does have insecurity issues like everyone else. He's critical of you because it shifts the focus off him. And even he's unaware of it.

Aries's Style

Aries people have a particular fashion sense, and it's usually not conservative. Styles range from funky to slick to fashionable and even odd, at times. They'll expect you to have your own. They want a mate to look good on their arm. That said, Aries women usually like distinguished-looking men. Though she herself may have a colorful style, she often likes a man who dresses in a conventional way. Aries men, on the other hand, admire a woman who can look feminine yet still sexy—with bold garments, such as leather pants and a jacket with a low-cut silk top, or a daring outfit, such as an off-the-shoulder, tight but tasteful dress.

🅴 Fact

Aries is practical. He also usually leans toward the tidy side of the spectrum. If a would-be mate of an Aries man ever left lipstick on the pillowcase, for instance (and he's not in love), it would be the quick cause of a no-nonsense dismissal.

All in all, Aries tends to be a little selfish. You may want to look elsewhere for a compliment on how stylish your outfit is, though subtle flattery works on Aries himself. If you want to know how you look, ask someone else.

In short, Aries likes a mate with bold moves. He likes to be surprised. Take him to a place he's never heard of, spend a little money, and be outrageous. Too much mystery will not cause Aries to stall. He'll follow you to the ends of the earth to conquer you. Don't let him—at least, not right away.

The Sex Issue

This leads us to the topic of sex. Aries has a hearty appetite for it and is also quite good at the sport. He'll expect you to know your way around the bedroom, too—though he may have to convince himself first that it's more than just another roll in the hay. Press too hard or pressure to move ahead too quickly, and Aries will beat a hasty retreat to the door. Because he's intuitive, he'll happily let you manipulate him with sex, but only if it's his will at the moment. Aries eventually thinks ahead to the long term, even if his attentions waver at any given second. So find a good balance with this exciting, unpredictable creature, and do read on.

Pillow Talk: Signs in the Bedroom

The key to keeping a sex life spiced up with the Ram includes providing satisfaction in every way but always keeping a little enticement waiting. If you bore Aries, in or out of the bedroom, the skid marks she'll leave won't be the only sign that she's not coming back. Try telling her you have a secret sexual maneuver that you'll just have to show her later. She'll do her best to get you back into bed. And remember, Aries likes to at least think she's in control at all times, even in the most intimate and compromising of positions.

The Secret Aries Man

What to do with a male Ram? You've got your work cut out for you. Aries men mostly prefer rough and tough over slow and sultry—they just don't have the patience. But they do know the right things to whisper into your ear. So if you're the type who likes a man to take charge and dominate you in bed, here's your guy.

The Aries Lover

Unfortunately, the typical Aries man can be egocentric in bed, too. But that's okay. There's one way to remedy this: Put an end to it immediately. In other words, don't wait a year to let this problem slip out in a verbal fight. (Aries will be devastated by the mere hint that he's been doing something wrong in the sack—though he probably won't believe it.) The truth is, the Aries man may be more wrapped up in his own needs, but he'll

be more than happy to meet yours, too. He just has to understand what those requirements are, and that means you have to
clue him in. Speak up!

🅴❗ Alert

> Strangely enough, an Aries man will be up front about
> what he doesn't like . . . but he doesn't necessarily want
> you to be! Aries is sensitive; he has thin skin. If you repri-
> mand him, make sure to do it gently.

Bedroom Play

When it comes to bedroom play, Aries likes to try everything
once. If he hints or talks outright about trying a little ménage à
trois, chances are, he plans on doing it anyway, with or without
you. Aries men take their own words seriously. He might tell you
it's getting late and "we'd better get home now or I'll be too tired
to make love." If he says it, it's a sure bet he means it. Aries men
should be believed when they say something, in bed or otherwise. Heed the warning and adjust accordingly. Are you ready
for the male Ram?

The Secret Aries Woman

Like her male counterpart, the female Ram loves to get
attention but needs a good challenge. Compliment her excessively (in the beginning) and you're making a mistake. She'll
like you and enjoy your company, but she'll never go to bed with
you. Don't be her personal throw rug. She'll walk all over you
and leave you out to dry. She wants a strong man—one who will
stand up to her but who will allow her to take the lead.

Note that there's a difference here between allowing her to
and letting her do what she wants. An Aries woman will know

when you're controlling her. If you're "allowing" her, she'll respect you more and believe you've got power. If you're "letting" her get away with things, she'll push the envelope further, thinking you're too weak to keep her. Then she'll go looking for another man worthy of her affections.

🅔❗ Alert

Even though you should never go overboard with an Aries woman, if she's lacking the attention and ego-soothing words she expects from you, she will look elsewhere. Keep on your toes to please a Ram. Balance is the key, always leaving a little mystery in the pocket.

Bedroom Escapades

Here's the rub. Like other Fire signs, Aries will expect her man to be superhuman in the bedroom. Outside, she wants to be the dominant force. In bed, though, she wants her man to take the lead (mostly). Though she believes herself to be in total control at all times, she surreptitiously wishes for an experience that will make the earth shake, causing her to lose it.

Like the Aries man, an Aries woman is a little wild and curious enough to try out all new sexual adventures, positions, and exploits. A soft, slow, sweet lovemaking session every night will only irk an Aries woman—she'll be left with something similar to a metaphorical itch. She'll want to scratch it. And that, of course, will leave you in the dust.

Keeping the Excitement

She'll look for a man who's not googly-eyed over her. An Aries woman wants to respect and look up to you as a confident he-man. In fact, telling an Aries woman that you love her too soon is a sure way to get her out the door. Chances are, she won't be back. This woman is all burning passion and fire, and she needs the same in a sexual mate.

Sun Love Matches

The typical Aries woman has more tact than an Aries man. Though she can be brutally honest, she's a little better at holding back random not-nice words and thoughts than her male counterpart. Because of this, she can get along with more signs than the Aries man. But the Aries woman is more selective. Both genders fall in love quickly and then sometimes realize they've made a grave mistake, though the Aries woman is more difficult to win over. Plus, an Aries woman won't tolerate a man dominating her, while an Aries man will just become amused with the notion. Let's break that down. Below are the different possible pairings for an Aries woman, the femme fatale.

Aries Man

Think rocket launchers and firecrackers. These two, when teamed up, are a force not to be beat. Turn them against one another, though, and they're likely to verbally fight to the end. An Aries man excites an Aries woman. There's no other man in the zodiac who can make her feel important the way he can. It's love at first sight, too, with great chemistry in and out of the bedroom. Unfortunately, both signs are impatient and restless—and both need a lot of security. Thankfully, an Aries man is willing to take a backseat to an Aries woman's antics. If they can be delicate with each other's feelings and give each other plenty of space without becoming too emotionally distant, this can be a good long-term affair—and an excellent chance for marriage, too. However, the pair must delegate who gets to win (Aries woman) and stick to it.

✅ Fact

Just to get an idea of how sexy an Aries man actually is, think charming: Sir Alec Guinness, Warren Beatty, Heath Ledger, Andy Garcia, Robert Downey Jr., Timothy Dalton (James Bond even!). Oh, and let's not forget Casanova, himself.

Taurus Man

True to his Bull sign, a Taurus man is stubborn. So is an Aries woman. A Taurus man can sometimes get a little too clingy and possessive for Aries (and even obsessive at times), but his bedroom prowess may impress her off the charts if there's chemistry. She also loves to be wined and dined by the Bull, though it may sometimes annoy her that he's only conditionally generous. In other words, he wants something for his efforts, and Aries won't put up with it: An Aries woman wants to go with the flow. Also, she'll provoke and frustrate Taurus to the limit . . . even if he'll only fall more in love with her for it (because he can't resist a good challenge). If she can stay still long enough for Taurus to win her, this can be a good friend partnership and maybe more. The potential is good for a passionate affair and perhaps marriage (but not necessarily recommended). This doesn't mean it can't happen if they both want it badly enough.

Gemini Man

A Gemini man is likely to win over an Aries woman right from the get-go. But even if Gemini is charming, attractive, and interesting to Aries, he may not be grounded enough to keep her. His antics will wear on her patience quickly, and the love affair may end. A Gemini man in bed, though, may have the kind of erotic sensuality and sustenance an Aries woman needs. His games will intrigue her, though he'll tend not to follow through—which may disappoint Aries. She's off in one direction; he's off in the other, making this a difficult love relationship to sustain. Though it's a quirky combination, they can have a good affair and possibly a long-term relationship, but it could wear thin after a while . . . unless Gemini remains solid for her.

Cancer Man

Believe it or not, these two together can be a successful couple. They're so different—like night and day. But the Cancer man has found his match in fire and passion. An Aries woman has it in bucketfuls. In fact, a Cancer man will be intrigued by an Aries woman and will want to know her secrets right away. If he's patient and doesn't push too hard, he'll eventually discover them.

Fact

Cancer men have substance to them—they're complex—and they'll want a mate who's emotionally deep, too: Tom Cruise, Harrison Ford, Tom Hanks, John Cusack, Prince William, and Tobey Maguire are all well-known Cancer men.

His calmness warms Aries and his hidden neuroses inspire her to come out with hers so that they can face them together. In some strange way, they balance each other—especially if Cancer is done playing. If the Cancer man is willing to wait at home while Aries goes out, this can be a good match. Sexually, the two are soul mates. This is a great long-term affair, with marriage a strong contender . . . providing Cancer and Aries are both emotionally mature.

Leo Man

The Leo man loves to strut his stuff, and this impresses Aries. Leo, too, will be unduly awed by her directness. He'll also be proud to carry a sexy, feisty Aries woman on his arm.

Unfortunately, a Leo man likes to be boss—and so does an Aries woman. Does he trust her judgment completely? Ah. There's the rub. In the bedroom, Leo's got the moves Aries has waited for. But he may be a little shocked when he's in the mood for some affection and Aries is halfway out the door. Leo can also be more sensitive than Aries, though both egos need to be pumped up endlessly. Passion-wise, the two are well matched. This union is a possible long-term affair and even has good potential for marriage, though it's not the best-case scenario unless the Leo man (king of the jungle) is ready to make the Aries woman his queen.

 Alert

A Leo man is only faithful for the right woman—one he knows can set boundaries for him (an Aries woman usually can). If she's cheating, on the other hand, instinctive Leo will sense it immediately and jump ship. His fierce pride simply won't tolerate the betrayal.

Virgo Man

The Virgo man is incredibly goal-oriented, and so is the Aries woman. While Aries is good at getting the ball rolling, Virgo won't stop until the task is done and done well. Virgo is great at managing Aries's affairs, but he'll be convinced she's not handling things correctly—namely, the way he would do it. Honestly, he just wants to help. However, there is a true meeting of the minds here and often a fatal-attraction type chemistry.

In addition, Aries can jump from subject to subject. This will irritate a Virgo man, who will feel like he's playing mental Ping-Pong. In bed, the Aries woman will be impressed by Virgo's attentiveness. The Virgo man will undoubtedly be attracted to the Aries woman's Fire, though he's not sure if he can control it. This worries him. Although this is a possible long-term relationship and also a very possible marriage, it could lead to problems later. The key here is to keep the communication and affection acceptable to both parties.

Libra Man

The Libra man is a poet. The Aries woman is wowed by this. Unfortunately, when the Aries woman realizes that his Libra "Fire" is more hypothetical, and that he hates any type of confrontation, she may go off looking for someone who can love her with more conviction. In and out of the bedroom, Libra is sexy, sensual, and charismatic. Aries is definitely attracted to him. Libra loves to keep his cool, but if there's one woman who can make him lose it, it's an Aries woman. (Libra doesn't necessarily like this.) In fact, Libra thinks Aries is a bit bossy. Though he'd love to take the risk, he'll most likely back off and look for easier prey. In bed, though, these two make erotic sex look tame. If Libra takes a chance on Aries, the two could make a good long-term relationship, with marriage possible. It's just not highly recommended unless it's with an Aries woman who's super-calm.

Scorpio Man

Speaking of great sex, the Scorpio man and the Aries woman can hole up for weeks on end and never see daylight. In bed, these two rock. Unfortunately, Scorpio's moodiness will affect Aries's natural playfulness, and the fighting will start. Scorpio is notoriously possessive, but Aries will take it more from her dark

mate than she would from Cancer or Virgo (out of respect and
a little fear).

❓ Question

Who's got the bigger temper?
The Scorpio man does, of course. He's the only one (besides
the Aries man) who can match an Aries woman's fury beat
for beat. Unfortunately, she may have a tough time figuring out the Scorpio man's manipulative strategies.

The Aries woman will be curious about Scorpio's well-hidden
secrets. If he discovers hers quickly: game over. However, Scorpio is more complex and can sometimes drag an Aries woman
down with his "I've-got-the-weight-of-the-world-on-my-shoulders"
attitude. If they find a good balance, and if Aries can leave Scorpio alone when he's stressed or feeling sorry for himself, this can
be a good couple with long-term relationship and even marriage
potential. It's recommended, however, only if Scorpio has his act
together and if Aries likes to live on the edge of her seat.

Sagittarius Man

These two can be great together. If there's one man in the
zodiac who won't bore the Aries woman, it's definitely a Sagittarius man. He'll even let her lead, though she knows he can take
the wheel if need be. And he's the he-man she may be looking
for—in bed. In fact, sex between these two can get out of hand.
It's wild, naughty, and exciting. There is one problem, though.
The Sagittarius man has absolutely no tact. He says it straight.
While the Aries woman admires this, she also can tire of it. Both
are charming, sexy, and fun. This is an okay love match, with
good odds for marriage . . . but only if the Aries woman learns

how to coo into his ear once in a while to sooth the savage beast (and if Sag can trust her).

Capricorn Man

Sometimes, these two are like kids in a candy shop. They're two of the three innocents of the zodiac (Leo being the third), and they can see things with optimism and wonder—if they choose. They love to laugh and joke, twenty-four hours a day, seven days a week—though Capricorn is much more black and white about things. Though it is said that the Capricorn man usually provides security to his mate, he finds a rough time with the Aries woman. Unfortunately for them, she wants to take the lead often, and this makes him turn the other way. In the bedroom, Aries likes Capricorn's straight-to-it style, but she wouldn't mind getting down and dirty, too. Though Capricorn would like nothing better, he'll never admit it. So the two might wind up having "polite" sex, all the while hoping they can find a better bed plan. These two have a shot at something long-term, with marriage possible, but not probable. Then again, never say never.

Aquarius Man

The Aquarius man is more detached and sometimes even more superficial than the Aries woman. What an odd feeling for Aries! In fact, he's even more unpredictable than she is—though this will inevitably turn her on and make her want the Aquarius man more. In truth, she's envious of the Aquarius lifestyle and his take-it-or-leave-it approach. His strangeness intrigues her, while his bold approach to life makes her feel she's found her soul match. In bed, the two may get restless and search for new ways together to relieve the boredom. Aries, though, is more fiery. The Aquarius man is more interested in performance than the Aries woman's lose-your-self-in-the-moment sex style. In the end, these two can have an interesting love match and a possible marriage, especially if this is with an Aries woman who is very "go with the flow." An unlikely match, but you never know.

Essential

Aquarius men are popular and may be quirky—but everybody loves them. In fact, they usually have a strange variety of friends who look for them constantly. This irks an Aries woman. She'll want a little attention, too, and maybe with a different crowd. If the Aquarius man is willing to let her have it, these two can be okay together.

Pisces Man

The Pisces man is utterly enthralled by the Aries woman. He won't necessarily know what to do with her or how to handle her. This is a shame because he has the power to control an Aries woman with his passion and sensitivity—he's deep enough to keep an Aries woman curious. He's also worldly, like she is. And he's a powerful soul: both romantic and expressive. Though the Aries woman's first wish will be to unravel the mysterious Pisces man, she may get quickly frustrated by Pisces's beat-around-the-bush strategy—and look elsewhere. He's curiously sedate for her. This can only be a winning love combination if the two take the time to really get to know each other and are willing to stick it out. A good love match and a decent marriage are possible, but only if the Aries woman has some "old soul" in her (like Pisces does) and he lets her call the shots.

Love Planets: Venus and Mercury

Sun sign combinations are just the tip of the iceberg. You'll want to take a closer look at other factors in your chart to understand the complete you. For example, your Venus is your real love sign—how you see love, what you look for in a mate, and how you deal with relationships. Mercury, on the other hand, is the planet of communication and intelligence. Good love matches depend on good communication . . . excellent Venus and Mercury compatibility are your foundations for it. First, check out the tables in the back of this book and discover if one of your other planets (or your mate's) is in Aries. Then read on.

Venus in Aries

You're not much of a homebody if your Venus is in this sign. On the contrary, you're always out and about—making love and war. You don't like to be controlled in love, and you get annoyed when a partner is nitpicky, pessimistic, or a general party pooper. Venus in Aries rarely makes for a faithful creature, though it depends with which Sun sign it's paired. These people love sex to be wild, exciting, and a little dangerous. To win over a person with Venus in Aries, play a little hard to get. Venus in Aries goes with Venus signs in Leo, Taurus, Aries, and Scorpio.

Mercury in Aries

You're smart, and you expect others to be. Though easily impressed, you'll change your mind about others in a flash—so watch out! Aries in Mercury is instinctively a good communicator and will always know the right way to approach a subject (so that they can win)—even if it is a bit devious. You'll entertain long debates only if you deem another person worthy of your time. Aries in Mercury is knowledgeable about many things. Good combinations with Mercury in Aries are Mercury in Sagittarius, Gemini, Aries, Virgo, and Taurus.

CHAPTER 2

Taurus

It's very possible a Taurus has charmed his way into your life at one time or another. Interesting, curious, playful, and sensitive, Bulls can make great friends, lovers, husbands, wives, and parents. Everyone knows the Bull is also not likely to take no for an answer, but what about his other, lesser-known traits? For a deeper understanding of sexy, sometimes unassuming Taurus, read on.

Can You Calm a Raging Bull?

1. **Name one thing that's not a Taurus trait 100 percent of the time.**
    A. Smart
    B. Curious
    C. Detail-oriented
    D. Attentive

2. **True or False: It's not a good idea to play hard to get with a Taurus.**
    A. True
    B. False

3. **If Taurus really likes you, how long should you wait until you sleep together?**
    A. Right away is okay if there's a connection.
    B. Third date is fine.
    C. A month or so.
    D. Until I'm ready . . . whenever that is.

4. **What is something that won't necessarily impress a Taurus?**
    A. Spirituality
    B. Status
    C. Cooking skills
    D. Intelligence

5. **Pick one thing that money does not mean for Taurus:**
    A. Security
    B. Freedom
    C. Luxury
    D. Happiness

6. **You have a fight with a Taurus right before bedtime. What should you do?**
   A. Wait till the next morning to work it out.
   B. Leave and call the next day or wait for a call.
   C. Try to seduce, hoping that will lighten the mood.
   D. Talk it out before sleeping.

7. **What are Taurus's favorite subjects to talk about?**
   A. Art and literature
   B. Business and marketing
   C. Science and politics
   D. All of the above

8. **What physical trademark should you use to spot a male Taurus?**
   A. Tall
   B. Broad-shouldered
   C. Thin
   D. A big nose

9. **What is the biggest turnoff for a Taurus?**
   A. Talks too much
   B. Can't budget finances
   C. Is a little neurotic
   D. Wears too much perfume/cologne

10. **What is a sure sign that Taurus is in love with you?**
    A. Offers words of affection
    B. Spends money on you and helps you with your bills
    C. Is very jealous of others around you
    D. Wants to spend a lot of time with you

Answers: 1. d, 2. b, 3. d, 4. a, 5. c, 6. d, 7. d, 8. b, 9. b, 10. b

The Conqueror

Put a Bull in a room full of women, and he's likely to work the entire place without breaking a sweat. He's a huge flirt—and whether or not he's good at it, he'll try—so you may not want to leave him alone in a room with your sexy single friend either. However, if he's committed to you, his moves will be all huff and bluff, most likely. In other words, a Taurus will take his relationship responsibilities seriously . . . most of the time. It's up to you to figure out if he's a Taurus you can trust or not. Know this, though: He's out to conquer, so if he's already won you over, he'll do his best to keep you. Unlike his predecessor in the zodiac, Aries, he's not just out for the game of it. He wants a long-term partner—marriage and the works. And if he hasn't already made you his, he's not likely to stop until he's done so.

I Want It and I'll Get It!

In this respect, Taurus can sometimes seem like a spoiled child who wants what he wants when he wants it. He can get obsessive if there's someone who won't give him the time of day. And once you're his, he's likely to think of you as a possession—a prize he's won. In other words, he'll be jealous and quite possessive if you're given to flirting, even for fun.

Both Taurus men and women scorned are like eyes of a storm—seemingly quiet while creating chaos around them on all sides. You won't want to make a Taurus angry. He'll lash out at you, perhaps even saying nasty things. If you've wronged him once, he probably won't give you another chance to do it again. He'll take his cards and lay them out on someone else's table.

Secret Traits

So there you have it. Taurus, both men and women, are charmers and great talkers. They have a wide range of interests and are—many of them—avid readers. Most Taurus people keep up with politics and international news. Another thing not widely known about Taurus is that he has to fall in love with your mind. While his body may tell him otherwise, it's not enough for you to be attractive and desirable to him. He's also on the look-out for a partner who can keep up with him both mentally and physically. Respect is important to him.

Alert

Like Cancer (though perhaps in a different way with Taurus), the Bull wants security above all—both financially and emotionally. If he feels he can't trust you, he won't waste his time investing his feelings in you. With Taurus, always do the right thing from the start.

Actually, Taurus is the most physical sign of the zodiac—in bed. Though Taurus is a natural sportsman, like Aries and Sagittarius, his sensuality in the bedroom is highly attuned. Like Scorpio, who is sexually instinctive but less romantic and more intense, Taurus has a sexual appetite heartier than all other signs. He also needs to dominate, both between the sheets and out. But he's more into the service aspect of making love: With this man, your needs will always come before his own.

You Can't Hurry Love

Here's a sign who likes to take her time with things. She'll want you to be totally devoted to her, but she wants the freedom to make up her mind about you when she's ready. If a Taurus feels she is being rushed in a relationship, she'll get even more stubborn and absolutely won't budge. For her, love must be a process: the wooing, the getting-to-know, the coming-to-terms, the agreements and disagreements, the commitment, and the final step—marriage. Taurus can sometimes be in a relationship for years before actually getting to the altar.

The Old-Fashioned Type

In fact, Taurus people are the most old-fashioned of the zodiac. They're gallant. A Taurus woman will wait for you for months, if need be (if she's in love . . . or headed there). Unfortunately, this can work the other way, too. Go to bed with her too quickly—or even drink too much alcohol in front of her—and she'll judge you for it. Sometimes you may think that if you sat her down with one of your grandparents, the two could go on for hours about "kids these days."

❗ Alert

Make sure to listen when your Taurus mate talks about others. She's giving you clues about how she wants you to behave—what you should and shouldn't do, and what she considers "proper." In this way, you'll get a better idea of what your Bull is all about.

The Art of Attraction

It would be easy to assume that because Taurus men and women sometimes like a good old-fashioned courtship, you should be polite, easygoing, and affectionate with them. Here's a tip: not so. Though it's wrong to play games in love, perhaps, Taurus actually needs affection but also a little space (pulling away) and verbal teasing in the beginning to get the ball rolling.

In other words, if you come off easy and sweet, your Taurus will not think you're a prize worth winning: He's a conqueror, remember? Just make sure you always listen to the Bull. If he feels like he's not being heard, he's sure to get cranky.

The Long Haul

Whether or not you'd actually be good for him is not the point. Taurus has a hard time choosing a partner who's right for him. He tends to set his sights on someone more for the security (or the challenge) than for suitability. In fact, the more you tell a Taurus you're not right for him, the more likely he is to pursue you. As mentioned, Taurus has a tough time with "no."

🅴 Alert

If you want to get a Bull, don't play coy—think mother or father figure. Be nurturing and then pull away and reprimand Taurus (in the beginning). He'll quickly become attached and aim to win your affections.

When they don't cut themselves off emotionally, Taurus makes for a wonderful mate, father, or mother. Sometimes when the Bull is out for something, he holds tight to the security itself, and that becomes his definition of real love. Instinctively, though, he knows how to draw someone to him and how to get someone's affections. True, this is done by simply pulling away. Taurus goes off to sulk, and his partner, who's used to the constant affection, goes after him. But Taurus always provides the constancy that he himself craves for family and will eventually attempt to ensure everyone's happiness around him. He loves sweetness, too . . . every little bit.

The Little Stuff Counts

Taurus likes expensive, tailored clothes but doesn't necessarily like to wear them. However, he likes you to be dressed well (monkey see, not do). Like their ideals, they tend to lean toward the conservative side. For a woman, a little sexy is okay, as long as it isn't overdone in public. Though the Taurus man may seem to like it, he'll be silently wondering if you've dressed like this for him or for everyone else in the room. Be safe and take a sweater along to drape over that sexy black dress. This will impress Taurus. In private, however, the sky's the limit.

Master of Perception

Here's another kicker. Taurus is very good at discovering your little secrets—the ones he's interested in. He'll play it cool and subtly get the information out of you. Then he'll file it away and use it as ammunition when he needs it. On the surface, Taurus comes off as calm and noncritical, going along with whatever you say. Deep down, though, he's playing all kinds of scenarios in his head.

The Money Factor

Here's how to get rid of a Taurus quickly: Tell him you have a little bit of a spending problem. You try to manage your finances well, and you try not to spend even though you're in debt, but you just can't seem to stop. Don't be surprised if Taurus's head spins around and rolls off his shoulders. Actually, chances are that you won't get any reaction. As mentioned before, Taurus is great at hiding distaste. Eventually, it will come out, but not usually in the moment.

Don't be surprised if the Bull romances you with expensive theater tickets or a candlelight dinner for two at the hottest restaurant in town. Because money is so important to Taurus, he'll think it's important to you, too. Unfortunately, though, Taurus's generosity does not normally stem from an infectious need to give (as it does, let's say, with Leo). Taurus expects something for his efforts.

 **Essential**

Many famous astrologers characterize Taurus as material-istic. In truth, money for Taurus is not as much for luxury as it is for security. For Taurus, money is freedom, freedom is security, and security is happiness.

Pillow Talk: Signs in the Bedroom

Getting Taurus into bed is not always easy. Taurus wants to make love—not just have sex—if she's really interested. And she'll have to be in serious like or love (most of the time) to do that. It's important here to remember that Taurus often falls in love with partners who are not in love with her.

Making love to a Taurus is an art. She's not interested solely in the final outcome. Foreplay is genuine and an important prelude to the final act. She'll instinctively know how to warm you up, too. Both Taurus men and Taurus women are true sex hedonists—they wrote the book. Below are the differences between seducing a Taurus man and the female Bull.

The Secret Taurus Man

The Taurus man does, indeed, take himself a bit too seri-ously. The weight of the world is on his shoulders, and it's up to him to judge everyone. The whole financial security thing is not a joke—Taurus, no matter how much he's in love, will run away from a partner if he believes she has spending or debt problems. That said, one thing that will help you seduce the male Bull is to spend money on him (at the same time making clear, of course, that doing so does not cause you even the slightest hardship). Take him to an expensive restaurant, or do the opposite. Take him to a less expensive restaurant and show him how good you are at budgeting. He'll appreciate it.

Alert

Though patience is one of Taurus's identifying traits, he'll react with quick, determined impatience if you threaten his sense of constancy—financially or otherwise. When this happens, make amends immediately. And don't do it physically. Repair the problem with words.

The Right Approach

The Taurus man will withdraw physically faster than any other sign. If he's hurt, you'll know it right away. He's sensitive. Also remember that Taurus gets a bit obsessive and has a tendency to sink into a depressive state when he's angry or feels he's been betrayed.

Don't try to woo a Taurus back to bed to make it up to him. He'll be offended. Instead, deal with the issue right away and don't go to sleep mad. If he has time to dwell on things, he'll be worse off the next day and the day after that. Once you've done your job, though, and Taurus forgives you (a difficult task!), you'll be surprised by how fast he'll warm right back up.

Making Love

In bed, these men love to bite and be bitten. They love all earthy, sensual qualities of lovemaking. Rub his neck to get him in the mood—it won't take long. Here's a tip: Though the Taurus man needs to dominate in bed, he feels strong and confident enough in his abilities to take direct orders. In fact, when a male Bull is told what to do in bed, it turns him on. He may even ask. Remember that he is service-oriented. He'll want you to "finish," like every other project he takes on in life. And the Taurus man will do everything he can to get you there.

 Fact

> Physically, Taurus men are usually broad-shouldered and can sometimes be stocky. They love to eat and to watch a woman eat, too. A little extra meat on a woman is not usually a problem for the average male Bull.

The Secret Taurus Woman

She's strong and sensual and very stubborn. If you push too hard or too fast, she'll balk. Vulgarity is a huge turnoff for her. Though she seems to be even more aggressive and modern in her approach to sex than her male counterpart, she's just as old-fashioned, strangely. In other words, she'll tempt you and tease you into bed, but she's secretly hoping you'll be man enough to stop and tell her you want to wait for the right moment. This will prove that you really care for her.

Stability Seeker

Though the Taurus man sometimes spins in circles trying to make enough money to appease his insatiable hunger for security, the Taurus woman intuitively knows how to earn it and keep it. She'll also look for a very stable provider—wealth can be an aphrodisiac for her. True, she'll also fall in love with a man who's not rich rich, but she'll never settle down with a man who can't take care of her and her future brood. She looks forward to being a parent if she can make it happen; she has an earthy, nurturing instinct that comes out. If she wants to, let her mother you a little.

e? Question

What is a great date for a Taurus woman?
Anything that makes her feel pampered. Take her out to a beautiful restaurant to wine and dine her. If she lets you into her house (a sure sign that she likes you; Taurus is territorial), cook for her. She may even fall for you.

Emotional/Physical Connection

Like the male Bull, the female Bull, unfortunately, gets attached to circumstances and misses out on emotions. In other words, her feelings are directly linked to the relationship in terms of what it can give her (security) instead of what she really needs (genuine love and getting to know the man behind it all).

She, too, can get a bit obsessed with unrequited love and can quickly fall into a depressive state. Sometimes bed may be the only way to reach her when she becomes emotionally distant and talking doesn't help.

The Proper Treatment

The Taurus woman also likes to bite and be bitten. She tends to shy away from very lean, skinny men. She wants to feel protected, and a big, hulking man is what she's likely to look for. Also, she may go for men who are well endowed. A Taurus woman can go for a little wildness in bed, but she also likes it sweet and slow. Focus on her neck, her buttocks, the back of her legs, and her chest; stay away from her stomach.

Sun Love Matches

Taurus, both man and woman, looks for a mate who will help keep an outwardly calm, tranquil appearance. Inside, they're often roiling with self-doubt and confusion. They shy away from partners who contest their way of handling things and try to dominate them (some Fire signs), as well as those who give too much ambiguity and who like to pick a fight with them for fun (some Air signs). Following are the love sign combinations with the female Bull.

Taurus Man

Physically, sexually, morally, and idealistically, these two make a great match. They share the same sense of commitment and family responsibility, and both want the security that they can give each other. This can be a great long-term relationship, with marriage probable . . . but only if the Taurus woman can let the Taurus man lead completely. This is a tough order, to be honest.

ⓔ✸ Essential

Both male and female Bulls are unnaturally stubborn, with a fondness for playing leader. The Taurus woman can sometimes be insensitive to the Taurus man's needs—and the Taurus man, too: to hers. Who's running this dictatorship?

Gemini Man

With a Gemini man, the Taurus woman won't know whether she's coming or going. This will drive her crazy. In fact, she may just develop an unhealthy attachment to the sense of excitement Gemini gives her. She also expects him to be more ambitious and career-oriented. For Gemini, this is too much pressure.

Intellectually, the two are well matched. In bed, both are sensual, but Gemini is more fascinated with the fantasy than with the reality of it. They might have a good affair, even a possible long-term relationship, but marriage isn't likely unless the Gemini man can get his act together and not drive her completely bonkers (and vice versa).

Cancer Man

The Cancer man can start off shy. If the Taurus woman doesn't come on too strong, he'll eventually open up to her. Both want a beautiful home and to spend lots of quiet time there. Sexually, these two are a good match if the female Bull doesn't order the Crab around too much. Both crave trust and are possessive and jealous. If their mood swings don't clash too much, and the Taurus woman can stay sensitive to Cancer's needs, the two can have a decent long-term relationship. They can also possibly have a marriage, albeit one with potentially plenty of problems . . . the Cancer man is sensitive and the Taurus woman never seems to read from the idealistic script Cancer has planted in his head.

Leo Man

The Taurus woman is completely taken in by the Leo man's exuberance and good looks. Unfortunately, although the Leo man knows how to make money, he also knows how to spend it. This worries the Taurus woman, who'd rather build a nest egg than go out to dinner every night. Sexually, these two are an incredible match. The Taurus woman excites the Leo man, and the female Bull loves that he is adventurous, intense, and playful in bed. This is a possible long-term relationship but not a probable marriage, unless the Leo man is so terrified of losing the Taurus woman that he treats her like fine threads of gold.

Virgo Man

Taurus and Virgo can go together. Spiritually, they get along and make each other laugh. They're also both insightful and determined—accomplishing whatever tasks they put their minds to. But the two of them are stubborn as well. If the Virgo man would stop being righteous with the Taurus woman, love-making for these two can be erotic, wild, and intense. Taurus is also wowed by Virgo's strange ideas and know-how when it comes to business and making money. She trusts him. This can be a good long-term partnership, with marriage a good possibility, though not highly recommended due to their ups and downs: Some couples of this match could make the scariest roller coaster look like a breeze. They both need to lighten up. Laughter and flexibility in tough situations is the key for these two to work.

Libra Man

If there's one thing the Libra man loves, it's beauty. And the Taurus woman is always beautiful in some way. They rarely fight because they both detest confrontation, though it's in Taurus's nature. However, Taurus is just holding back something important while Libra quickly dismisses and forgets.

 Fact

In terms of commitment, a Libra man and a Taurus woman flounder around on all fronts: relationship, jobs, and so on. If they can come to more resolute decisions, they make a great team.

If confrontations do happen, they're frequently solved in bed. Sexually, these two can move mountains, though Taurus likes to have sex more often than Libra. Taurus and Libra together make for a probable long-term relationship with a good chance for marriage if the Taurus woman doesn't weigh Libra down and Libra can handle Taurus's confrontational nature when it eventually comes out.

Scorpio Man

The two together are so intense, passionate, and deep that people around them sometimes feel they've just entered a minefield—or a Greek tragedy. Both have a tendency to feel a bit sorry for themselves, and they're both moody. If they can strike a good balance and not be so dramatic, they can be so good together that it's scary. In bed, their sensuality and sense of adventure reach new heights—though Scorpio, secretly, would prefer to lead a bit more. These two can have a probable long-term relationship and a probable marriage as well, but only if the Taurus woman doesn't become too predictable for the Scorpio man.

Sagittarius Man

The Sagittarius man is pensive, and the Taurus woman likes this. She admires his ability to do anything he wants and wishes she could be more open to the adventures he experiences firsthand.

Essential

Unfortunately, many Sagittarius men are too modest about their abilities and don't ask for enough compensation for their work. This bothers Taurus. She also can be easily hurt by his quick, honest tongue (until she understands that his words of love are also sincere).

Though Sagittarius will take the backseat sometimes to Taurus's desire to lead, he still believes he knows best and can be sarcastic about it, too. In bed, these two are good as long as Sagittarius can let himself feel the emotions that go along with the lovemaking. This is a possible long-term partnership, not a probable marriage. It's not a suggested one, but it's been done with success if the two really want it.

Capricorn Man

Capricorn is likely to fall in love with the Taurus woman. It seems she's the one he's always searched for. Unfortunately, they do have their differences. Even when the two don't want conflict, they get into fights constantly over issues of trust or money, and sometimes over absolutely nothing. Also, the Capricorn man likes to feel like he's in control. The Taurus woman shakes his stable ground. In bed, the Capricorn man can be more interested in what the act itself signifies than in his own sensuality. If these two can find a good balance, though, this can be an okay long-term partnership, with marriage a possibility. Again, "balance" is the operative word.

Aquarius Man

This is a real case of "opposites attract." You won't find a stranger couple—they're odd together, and yet it seems to work. The Aquarius man brings out the wildness in the Taurus woman, and she loves this about him. Though both can be incredible flirts, the Taurus woman worries a bit that the Aquarius man will stray—and he might. But if there's one who can keep him faithful, it's the female Bull. Also, the Taurus woman gets mad at the Aquarius man's calm, cool, "go-with-the-flow" attitude (about work, even). These two also have a superficiality hurdle to get over, which requires them to put their priorities into place. Sexually, they're both adventurous and can have fun in bed. This is a probable relationship and a very possible marriage, especially if the Taurus woman is not too focused on money-making and the Aquarius man can keep his feet on the ground.

ⓔ Essential

Aquarius men like strangeness in the bedroom. If the Taurus woman can let go and loosen up completely, the Aquarius man will be more taken by her. Aquarius needs to be wild and, many times, wouldn't mind experimenting with sex toys.

Pisces Man

The Taurus woman is drawn to Pisces's sense of tranquility, his emotional depth, and his instinctive ways. She should trust him more on his judgment of people. Taurus, though, is able to relax and be herself with a Pisces man even if she can't always take the criticism he doles out. Fortunately, Pisces knows how to word his views just the right way. In bed, the Pisces man lets the Taurus woman take the lead, and the two play well together. If they stop manipulating each other at times, this pair can make for a possible long-term relationship and a marriage with fireworks. However, how long can you go with things always so hot and somewhat bothered? That's the question.

Aries Man

The Aries man sweeps the Taurus woman off her feet. The two are social, but the Aries man needs more diversity than the Taurus woman, who wants simple constancy, not chaos. The issue of trust comes up between them, a lot. Aries is not half as possessive or emotionally reckless as the Taurus woman—who's strong, but can go half-mad with the wrong partner. Problem is, Aries knows just how to push her buttons to hike those negative traits up a notch. Also, the Taurus woman is so wowed by the Aries man, she doesn't stop to think if she's in love with him or just in love with the idea of him. In bed, things are great. Chances are that this is a possible long-term relationship but not a good idea for marriage . . . although, again, stranger things have happened.

Love Planets: Venus and Mercury

If Venus or Mercury is in Taurus for you or for your mate, make sure to read the entire Taurus chapter. Every nuance of Taurus is included and will help you understand the sign and its influences more comprehensively. Venus and Mercury dates are at the back of the book. Read the charts and match yours accordingly. Taurus in any person's chart will always add an obstinate nature, a need for status or security—financially. For more precise information, read on.

Venus in Taurus

Though you may like to travel, coming home to a stable, tranquil environment is what you always look forward to. Family is very important, and you strive to be a good parent. You search for a love partner who will give you security and who will be faithful. However, it would be wonderful if he were a great cook, too! Infidelity is something you absolutely won't tolerate. When other people tell you about your choice of love mate, listen. They sometimes know better about what's best for you. Venus in Taurus goes well with Venus in Taurus, Gemini, Libra, Pisces, and Scorpio.

Mercury in Taurus

Intellectually, you know how to express yourself. You may be drawn to jobs of a more technical nature. If not, your artistic edge could come out in another way, such as in writing. People are impressed with the way you handle yourself professionally, but you have a tough time with authority and don't necessarily stay long in any office job. Working freelance may suit you more. You may be interested in the way things work. You're also realistic and practical, and though a touch romantic, despise a mate who seems to live in a fantasy world. You wouldn't mind letting someone change your mind for you, but nobody can ever quite do it. Mercury in Taurus goes well with Mercury in Taurus, Capricorn, Libra, Scorpio, and Pisces.

CHAPTER 3

Gemini

Gemini is so crafty, so devilish . . . so delightful—and just when you think you've really gotten to know him? You could be mistaken. Gemini is the most unpredictable of all the signs in the zodiac. In fact, the only thing you can count on with the Twin is that you can't really count on anything. In this chapter, learn the tricks of the Twin and Gemini's deepest, darkest secrets.

Can You Get to the Heart of the Gemini Twin?

1. **What is the worst way to get Gemini's attention?**
   A. Being silly
   B. Flirting directly
   C. Flirting with others
   D. Being playful

2. **What kind of personality will not impress a Gemini?**
   A. A social butterfly
   B. A jet-setter
   C. A homebody
   D. A workaholic

3. **Gemini is stranded for a few hours in a large room with only four people. Who would Gemini choose to hang with?**
   A. Someone funny
   B. Someone smart
   C. Someone weird
   D. Someone interesting

4. **Which of these is Gemini most likely to flirt with?**
   A. A person Gemini finds attractive
   B. A baby
   C. A puppy
   D. All of the above

5. **When Gemini tells a story, the Twin usually:**
   A. Embellishes
   B. Tells it straight
   C. Makes it up out of nowhere
   D. Makes it short, leaving out details

6. **If someone tried to steal a bag or a briefcase from Gemini, what would the Twin probably do?**
    A. Yell and get people around to help
    B. Immediately call the police
    C. Run after the mugger
    D. Curse a lot, then deal with it

7. **Name one negative trait of Gemini.**
    A. Picky
    B. High maintenance
    C. Boring
    D. Fickle

8. **What is a good trait that Gemini is known for?**
    A. Charming
    B. Grounded
    C. Composed
    D. Fair

9. **What does Gemini not like when it comes to sex?**
    A. Sensual moves
    B. Experimentation, out of the box
    C. Naughtiness: Everything's pretty much game.
    D. No talking: Shh . . . silence is golden

10. **How quickly can Gemini get over a broken heart?**
    A. A few months to a year—or more; then she never looks back.
    B. She never gets over it.
    C. A couple of years or less . . . but she'll take it out on the next person she dates.
    D. Love, with Gemini, can always be rekindled.

The Born Storyteller

No one can tell a story like Gemini. She'll have everyone in the room hanging on her every word. Of course, every tale is a little bit better when it's tweaked for consumption: exaggerated and embellished. That's what's expected from Gemini. It's part of her charm.

Gemini can easily charm people of the opposite sex, true. But she'll also flirt with anyone who happens to be in front of her—friends, children, senior citizens, even animals. She does it because it's second nature to her. In fact, Gemini will always have a horde of fans at any given time.

Fact

Gemini needs to be adored and considers it her birthright. She knows she's sexy and that others dig her—and she's always prepared to use her assets to help her with any situation.

Moody Outbursts

Gemini gets bored easily. She changes her mind constantly and expects you to keep up. She can be unrealistic, and she frequently unwittingly sabotages close, personal relationships. She also gets distracted when the conversation doesn't revolve around something she's interested in.

Gemini, you should know, can display a bit of a violent nature if she feels betrayed. Chances are, she's only out for the drama of it—but do yourself a favor and expect to have the phone hung up on you if she's angry. Don't worry, though. Gemini also forgives faster than any other sign. She just won't let you know that and may make you suffer for a while.

Alert

Don't try to make up with hotheaded Gemini when she's angry—she'll cut you down to size. Give her some breathing room and time to think. She'll come back to you with an apology (if she's wrong) the next day.

Twin's Generous Side

Shortcomings aside, Gemini is one of the more generous signs. She gives great advice and knows exactly what to say to cheer you up—even if her words are a bit unorthodox. Really, Gemini is a great friend and gives every bit of her soul to a love relationship. Actually, she sometimes gives too much of herself. She's confident and will lay her cards on the table, perhaps a little too soon. But that doesn't seem to bother anyone who's falling for a Gemini. Instead, most members of the opposite sex feel lucky to have her. She's a wild card—funny, exciting, and beautiful—and yet sometimes off her rocker (in a good way). True, she can even be flaky at times, but one thing is for sure: No one is ever bored with the erratic Twin.

Split Personality

So how is it possible to predict what a Gemini will do next when he, himself, doesn't know? It's not easy. One moment he seems to like you; the next he's ignoring you, chatting away with his buddy. What should you do? Well, for starters, remember that in terms of needing a good challenge, Gemini is as bad as Aries. Aries, though, is more interested in the chase, whereas Gemini is curious about the possibilities. Gemini loves to always leave a few options open. The excitement of

"Will I or won't I?" always plays a part in the Twin drama of the moment.

e? Question

How do you get Gemini's attention?
In the beginning, don't flirt too much. Flirting indicates you're interested. In Gemini's mind, he's already conquered you. Show him you can have a good conversation and talk to others. If he wants you, he'll find you and make his play.

The Love Game

The saying "split personality" really can apply to Gemini. He's not easy to figure out right away, and you'll hurt your head trying. Just when you feel like the two of you have clicked, he'll pull away. He can even seem a little obsessive at times, but he's nothing like Cancer, who can get out-of-control nuts with his thoughts. For him, it's all part of the love game. Here are a few examples:

- Gemini romances you all night, then leaves without saying goodbye.
- Gemini is always there for you, but the one time you need him the most, he's off resolving another "situation."
- Gemini picks a best buddy to hang around with, then tells you about his friend's shortcomings.
- Gemini dates the least appropriate person within a mile's radius—especially when people tell him not to.
- He calls you ten times in one day, then tells you you're being insecure if you ever do the same.

As you can see, it's not easy keeping a Gemini blissful. But as a lover, Gemini knows no bounds. He's extremely affectionate to his one and only—when he gets around to choosing her.

🗸 Fact

Gemini likes to be out and about. He needs to be social. If he's all work and no play, he's not a happy camper.

Gemini can't go for a long time without being in love. He doesn't like to stay alone. You will almost never find two- or three-month stretches when the most exciting entry in his smartphone's calendar reads "Get up, feed dog, go to work, come home, eat dinner, go to sleep."

The Twin's View on Work

Most Geminis, in fact, don't really like to work—unless they love their job and it gives them tons of freedom (a rarity). They do it for a sense of dignity, and for money or prestige, but rarely because they actually enjoy it. When they do love it, it's a great thing. But for Gemini, work is usually a means to an end. Many Gemini women wouldn't mind taking off from work and having their husbands take care of them. Of course, they'd be bored in no time.

The Art of Attraction

Gemini practically oozes sex. Man or woman, Gemini has sex appeal that could conquer entire countries. In fact, if you want to have fun in an otherwise boring social situation, bring a Gemini along. She'll know exactly how to keep the conversation going.

 **Essential**

> Gemini can get along with anybody (if she's so inclined). If not, a verbal lashing or a little sarcasm might just be how a Gemini flirts. Read on to learn what makes a Gemini tick and how to get her hooked.

The Long Haul

Most Geminis get married later in life. They claim that they'd like to settle down and raise a family—yet they find either this or that wrong with their potential mates. Better still, they have long-term relationships with people they know are simply not suitable for the long haul. Chances are, though, they're more worried about what tomorrow will bring than what lies fifteen years in the future.

Gemini tends to fall in love with the person who makes her laugh. She's extremely witty and wants her partner to be, too. Remember that she's an Air sign, so she's got to be conquered first through her mind. She always goes for someone cool, daring, and exciting.

The Little Stuff Counts

Gemini women like to dress on the sexy side. At the very least, they'll wear something to go along with their fun, flirty personalities. Gemini men, on the other hand, are stylish and sexy no matter what they wear. They're not particularly conservative. They go along with the latest style, as long as it's not too trendy or weird. The Gemini man doesn't mind a bit of sexiness in his partner—as long as it's tasteful.

Showing Off

Gemini men and women both like to show off their partner on their arm. If a Gemini introduces you to all her friends, you should know she really likes you. Her friends are her lifeline. But love is always important to a Gemini. She falls in love quickly, it's true, but whether it's true love, only time will tell. If it's not, a Gemini will be out the door faster than you can say the word "fickle."

 **Essential**

Gemini men and women take great care in their appearance. A compliment will go a long way. In fact, you'll get extra points if you notice a new shirt, dress, or hairstyle.

The Big Spender

When it comes to money, Gemini tends to spend more money on his partner than on herself. She's usually generous and doesn't expect anything for it (except your constant devotion and loyalty!). As far as wanting something for her efforts, this is understandable.

Playing Games

When it comes to playing games, Gemini invented the rules. A less evolved Gemini will be a little needy, possessive, and manipulative. But in the end, she may still get what she wants. Beware, though, of a clingy Gemini. This tends to be the type who can get violent if provoked. A more evolved Gemini, on the other hand, will come close to giving the appearance of an Earth sign: grounded. She'll be interesting, fair, and emotionally balanced—a wonderful lover and partner.

Fact

Gemini is also open to mates of a different background, race, religion, and even age. It's not uncommon for a Gemini to date a person much older or much younger than she is.

Pillow Talk: Signs in the Bedroom

Gemini is definitely able to separate sex, love, flings, and real relationships. If he gets it in his mind that you're nothing more than a roll in the hay, he's not likely to change his mind and let it develop into something more meaningful. Gemini is also very sexual but not necessarily sensual (like Cancer). This means that slow, languorous sex is probably not on the menu for the evening.

Actually, Gemini goes for the strange and interesting in the bedroom. Nothing is out of bounds or considered taboo for some Geminis. Gemini also likes to be seduced. A conservative "let's have sex" line will absolutely not work on a Gemini. The Twin goes for a flirty, sexy smile and deep, dark eye contact. Gemini is an expert in the seduction category and expects you to be, too.

 Alert

Don't necessarily run away from a Gemini who's just insulted you! This is what he wants—he's testing you. Gemini men were the ones who pulled your ponytails in class. Strangely enough, it may be the one way he shows he likes you. Hit him up with a teasing remark back!

The Secret Gemini Man

The Gemini man, on the whole, doesn't know what he wants. If you look at a list of his past relationships, you may have a problem finding a particular pattern to his conquests. Instead, his ex-girlfriends only have one thing in common: They're all completely different. But one thing is true—either he walked away from the relationship first or they walked away, came back, and he turned them down when they did.

Seducing the Twin

As said before, Gemini really gets turned on with the mind. Serve up some good wine, make some good conversation, and demonstrate you understand who the people around you are. That will impress a Gemini man and make him like you more. There's not much you can do to seduce a Gemini man into bed, though. He has decided before the evening even started whether he plans to take you to bed.

Pleasure in Bed

Once in the bedroom, though, the Gemini man is adventurous and crafty. He's a fantastic kisser and likes doing it. He'll need to vary positions to keep his interest up. And Gemini can be a bit sexually selfish, too. This time, with encouraging words, you can guide Gemini to make him understand what you want. Gemini will pick up your cues easily.

The Secret Gemini Woman

She can be wild in bed. Once she's given herself to you, she'll expect all kinds of sexy moves and seduction. You'll feel like Gemini is grading you—and she is. Conservative positions don't necessarily tickle her fancy. She's looking for style, flair, and imagination.

Sex Talk

Sometimes she likes dirty talk in bed—other times, she might want you to just tell her how much "I want you" in her ear. Ask her what mood she's in. She'll tell you. Most Gemini women carry their verbal skills into the bedroom in some way, even if it's just to give an occasional "ooh" or "aah" to let you know you're doing just fine.

 Fact

> For the Gemini woman, great lovemaking is important. She'll leave a relationship that doesn't have it and stay way too long in a relationship that does.

The Gemini woman is more easily seduced than the Gemini man. Though she's probably decided before the night has started whether she'll allow herself to "trip the light fantastic" with you, she can be swayed with sexy conversation (including what you'd like to do with her if you got your way).

Alert

> Gemini women tend to be on the jealous side. Watch out! If she sees you talking to your ex at a party, not only will you miss out on getting lucky—you just might have first-rate drama on your hands.

Playing It Safe

Okay, so some Gemini women like to create scenes. Their tendency toward exhibitionism has a mind of its own. Did you ever see a man get a drink thrown in his face or a woman screaming at him at the top of her lungs in public? Chances are, it was a Gemini woman creating the chaos. It's best not to provoke a Gemini woman. Play it safe and keep her happy: Your time with her will remain copacetic.

Sun Love Matches

Gemini tends to fall for rogues, Casanova types, femme fatales, or lady-killers. The Gemini woman will always look for a "difficult" partner—one who has a sharp tongue and is not easy to control. She basically has two types of fans: one whom she can lead around and tell what to do, and one who will dominate her. The latter has a much better chance of winning her heart. Once she settles down, though, she usually finds the right balance. Read on to learn about the love-sign matches for the female Twin.

Gemini Man

These two like to gossip, play, and get into trouble together. They sometimes get into cat-and-dog fights only to turn around, kiss, and make up. Don't bother siding with one of them because they're more likely to forgive each other immediately and then consider you a traitor. In fact, they're each other's sounding board. Their connection is deep because it's based on the mind (and good sex). Unfortunately, neither is extremely adept at earning money and keeping it. They have great ideas, but they are likely to start a project and never finish it. However, these two make a probable long-term relationship and have a great chance for marriage, especially if someone in the family has deep pockets . . . and they could stop the constant bickering (sometimes it's foreplay for them, though).

Fact

Gemini signs will be instantly attracted to each other—even if it's only for a secret, steamy love affair. A good example of this would be Marilyn Monroe and President John F. Kennedy (both Geminis).

Cancer Man

These two can be manipulative and sneaky with a tendency to play dirty—and they actually like this about each other in a weird way. Things are definitely not boring between them. Unfortunately, Cancer doesn't always trust the Gemini woman on many levels. She flirts with others too much for his taste. She tells little fibs here and there, perhaps. The Cancer man could teach her many things, but the Gemini woman won't let him. Both can be possessive and moody, although Gemini can be quickly snapped out of a bad mood while Cancer can't. This bothers the Gemini woman. She also likes to go out on the town more than the Crab at times. In bed, both are adventurous, but Cancer wants Gemini to prove that her feelings run deeper than he suspects. This can be a long-term relationship but not a probable marriage, unless Gemini has suffered some hardships in life and can relate to sensitive Cancer.

Leo Man

The Leo man finds Gemini to be refreshing, exciting, interesting, and witty. No one can make Leo laugh like Gemini, and vice versa. Though he finds her incredibly amusing, he wonders if she's sincere. The two challenge each other, but Leo doesn't like liars, however harmless. If she's straight with him, they're good. Both know how to play the game and keep each other guessing.

Leo gives Gemini the kind of loyalty she needs, but a less evolved Gemini will have a hard time doing the same for the Leo man. She loves the fact that he's generous with money. In bed, things can be utter paradise or complete hell—depending on whether the two stay connected during the relationship. If they can, this may be a possible long-term partnership . . . and can be a good marriage as well (especially if this particular Leo man is as light and airy as the Gemini woman).

Virgo Man

It's difficult to be around these two when they bicker. Verbally, they can be cutting and harsh. In fact, if there's any man who can reduce a Gemini woman to tears, it's a Virgo man. She'll have to develop a thicker skin to be with him. Intellectually, though, these two can talk till morning. They know how to amuse one another, and Gemini likes Virgo's attentive, instinctive style in bed. Also, if Gemini can convince Virgo to give way to his natural sexual tendencies, these two can go for hours without coming up for air. Unfortunately, though, Virgo can sometimes bring out the worst in the Gemini woman. She'll purposely provoke and irritate him for the fun of it, and the relationship will end. This is a possible long-term relationship, but not a recommended marriage . . . unless Gemini is mature and doesn't get "needy" (in Virgo's eyes), and Virgo is willing to let go a little more.

Libra Man

Together, these two are wickedly mischievous. The Gemini woman is impressed with Libra's sense of style and flair. She loves his eyes and his long, sexy stares. She'll be curious to figure him out. Both like to be worshipped in bed and, though the sex can be masterful, the Libra man sometimes wishes the Gemini woman would be a little more soft and shy for him. This would make him more comfortable. This is a probable long-term relationship, and there's even a decent chance for marriage if the Libra man can "tame" the Gemini woman to his liking. However, how many Libra men are up for that?

eV Fact

Libra is not as cool and calm as he may seem to be. His silent treatments make her nervous and could make her a bit aggressive. Libra also likes to avoid conflict, while Gemini sometimes (unwittingly) searches it out.

Scorpio Man

When Scorpio falls, he falls hard. Otherwise, he's off playing. In the beginning, he'll give the Gemini woman the attention she needs. He'll call when he's supposed to and treat her like a queen. But this affection may dwindle after a while or even stop completely. The Gemini woman also doesn't have the means or the inclination to figure out Scorpio's hidden agenda. It may drive her nuts. The two can go in circles with verbal games. Also, Gemini can't stand Scorpio's bad moods. Scorpio, though, has just the right blend of passion and moves in bed for finicky Gemini. If she goes to bed with him, she'll keep coming back for more. They have a somewhat decent chance for a long-term relationship, and, if they marry, it could last a while—but Scorpio is always changing. Therefore, this tough guy looks for guidance when he lets his guard down later on . . . and Gemini may become too predictable and perhaps even self-absorbed (for him) when he does.

Sagittarius Man

The Gemini woman and the Sagittarius man sometimes make a great couple at first because when Sagittarius becomes quiet, Gemini keeps the conversation going. Good—and bad. Some Sag men don't like when a woman talks too much just for the sake of it. True, Gemini is a bit too flighty for Sagittarius's tastes, and he doesn't always trust her. She does amuse him, though—and he eats up her compliments. Unfortunately, the Gemini woman doesn't always take his advice, and this bothers him. She can also get possessive, which he also definitely doesn't like (though it's okay when he is). In bed, though, these two can create fireworks. If Gemini remains emotionally stable, it's probable they can have a long-term relationship and, beyond that, marriage is possible, though not necessarily highly recommended unless both are emotionally mature and can remain a united team.

Capricorn Man

The Capricorn man doesn't believe a single thing that comes out of Gemini's mouth—and he shouldn't. She purposely shocks him and provokes him for kicks. He's too easy a target for her. This combination really depends upon what the rest of Capricorn's chart looks like. If he is especially earthy, forget it. If he has a lot of Air and Fire, this can be an okay match. Gemini inspires Capricorn to make money and try new things. Capricorn, on the other hand, grounds Gemini. If he takes her seriously, these two can conquer worlds together. In bed, Gemini tends to be a bit wilder than the Goat, and she may grow tired of his more conservative approach to lovemaking. This can be a possible long-term partnership, but it's not a probable marriage . . . unless the two work together and have a lot of things to talk about—or simply tons of common ground.

🅔 Alert

The easiest downfall for Capricorn with Gemini is that the Twin likes to talk about the relationship (and maybe even the sex): Capricorn will avoid these conversations at all costs! This makes Gemini nervous. Eventually, this problem will fester and could become bigger (and more problematic) than the love partnership itself.

Aquarius Man

These two make a great team. Finally, the Aquarius man thinks, he has found a woman who excites him and can keep him on his toes. Though Aquarius is a bit more grounded than the Gemini woman, the two together can still get into plenty of mischief. Fun is a key word here. Laughter is another. They both have the same style in and out of bed. The Aquarius man, however, can sometimes be a bit too strange for Gemini (but she may just appreciate this, too). The Gemini woman seems somewhat out of control to the Aquarius man—only because he's more cerebral. If they stay away from superficial matters and get their priorities in order, this can be a good long-term relationship and a good marriage after that, perhaps . . . but it really depends on the combination of the two together and how grounded Gemini is. She does seem to irk Aquarius sometimes.

Pisces Man

These two make a strange pair, but it can work sometimes. Pisces is very quiet. Gemini does most of the talking. Pisces provides an outlet through which Gemini can experience the range of her emotions. Pisces has a lot to teach her, and Gemini is curious to learn from him: He may grow weary of this, though. If he stays strong and doesn't let Gemini play with his affections (or drive him nuts), they can be okay together. Pisces, though, is a bit more romantic in bed while Gemini is more spontaneous. This can be an interesting couple—both in and out of the bedroom. If Gemini doesn't get too clingy and Pisces too withdrawn, they have a possible long-term relationship in store, and then an okay chance for marriage. Frankly, though, it just depends upon what Pisces is willing to put up with for the sake of love (and vice versa).

Aries Man

The Aries man knows just how to get the Gemini woman interested. One look and she's hooked. Neither one likes to feel pressured or suffocated in a relationship. They both like going out, being social, and flirting. There's only one problem: Gemini does it for fun, while Aries means it (the contacts, the socializing, the flirting). If Gemini gets possessive, Aries will run the other way. In bed, these two can be a sexual miracle—fabulous lovers. If Gemini respects Aries's preferences for life and the way it should be lived, this is a probable long-term relationship with a good outlook for marriage. However, be forewarned: Let the drama begin. It just depends on what you're looking for.

Essential

Gemini's little outbursts might bother Aries, and he won't forgive her if she says something nasty to him. However, she won't take it back for a while. And when she does, it's usually done its damage.

Taurus Man

No matter how hard he tries to figure the Gemini woman out, he simply can't get what makes her tick. This will drive him nuts.

Just when he imagines things are going smoothly, she shows up late, once again, with a ridiculously flimsy excuse. He lets her get away with it because he can't stand fighting in public. He prays she won't make a scene. Sometimes he's embarrassed by her flamboyant sexual behavior (though he's secretly turned on by it). If Gemini lets him, Taurus can show her a thing or two in bed. Once she's gone to bed with him, Gemini won't easily let Taurus get away, and vice versa. Though this is a strange couple, they can definitely work: a possible long-term relationship . . . though marriage may be problematic unless both have their act together. There will be a lot of love, but some serious upheavals, too. If they go for it, the sky could be the limit.

Love Planets: Venus and Mercury

A Venus or Mercury in Gemini will give you a more inquisitive nature. It also gives you better verbal skills and a need to communicate, to be heard. Though Gemini is a good talker, he can be a good listener as well. Read on to find out how Gemini affects the stars and planets in your chart.

ⓔ Essential

Gemini's standards are high, requiring that any potential partners match his specifications almost point for point. Also, he won't give his partner any hints as to what he's looking for. He expects her to figure it out for herself.

Venus in Gemini

Though many astrologers say that a person with Venus in Gemini can be unfeeling and rationalizes too much, this is simply not so. You fall in love with love. You have plenty of emotions but don't know how to express them. Instead, you have protective barriers up because you've been burned once or twice and refuse to let yourself be burned again. In love, you can change your mind a number of times, but once you've picked a target, you attach yourself to it . . . him—(or her)! The person you want becomes a fixation. Instead of moping about, pining after him, though, you take the aggressive route and go after him. Once you have what you want, you may not be sure you want it, however. If you do, you'll dedicate your time solely to him. This is true of both men and women who have Venus in Gemini . . . Venus in Gemini matches with Venus in Gemini, Taurus, and Leo.

Mercury in Gemini

Though you're a great talker, your ideas are extreme and go from one end of the spectrum to the other. In fact, you love to be persuaded and may even fall in love with someone who can easily accomplish this almost impossible task. You have good timing and can tell a joke quite well once you get up the nerve to do it. In terms of work, you'd do well writing speeches or scripts for television or the movies. You may even be drawn to a partner who doesn't say a lot because you're convinced there's more to him than meets the eye. You're also not averse to telling a little white lie when "necessary." It's part of your diplomatic nature. However, you like to feel in your gut that your potential mate deserves your faith and trust before you actually give it. Mercury in Gemini can pair well with Mercury in Virgo, Aries, Gemini, Leo, and Taurus.

CHAPTER 4

Cancer

Cancer can almost seem like any other sign of the zodiac. Lucky him! He's got the dominance of a Fire sign, the sensitivity of a Water sign, the sensibility and practicality of an Earth sign, and even the ability to communicate like an Air sign. In this chapter, find out more about adaptable, energetic cardinal Cancer. He's not always the sentimental fool he's made out to be.

Who's in Control—You . . . or the Crab?

1. **What is the most important thing on this list to a Cancer?**
   A. Sense of humor
   B. Sexiness
   C. Trust
   D. Smarts

2. **What does Cancer think about an aggressive partner in bed?**
   A. Thumbs way up
   B. Doesn't like it
   C. Feels a little insecure about it
   D. Freaks Cancer out

3. **Most Cancers have a soft spot for:**
   A. Babies
   B. Charities
   C. Loyal friends
   D. All of the above

4. **What is not one of Cancer's flirt tactics?**
   A. Being playful
   B. Teasing
   C. Dominating
   D. Being coy

5. **Cancer may have a problem, at first, with:**
   A. Sex drive
   B. Commitment
   C. Having fun
   D. Talking too much

6. **Name one thing Cancer men are not:**
    A. Helpful
    B. Consistent
    C. Nurturing
    D. Funny

7. **How does a woman know for sure that a Cancer man is in love?**
    A. He calls her constantly.
    B. He lets her meet his mother.
    C. He makes hints about it.
    D. He marries her.

8. **If a Cancer really likes you, what is a date Cancer may do to impress?**
    A. Cook for you
    B. Take you out on the town dancing
    C. Splurge on a nice meal out
    D. Take you to a fun amusement park

9. **What style does Cancer use when trying to put the moves on?**
    A. Direct
    B. Indirect

10. **What is Cancer really looking for most in the long term?**
    A. An equal partner
    B. A sensuous lover
    C. An amazing friend
    D. A breadwinner

Answers: 1. c, 2. a, 3. d, 4. c, 5. b, 6. b, 7. d, 8. a, 9. b, 10. a

The Expansive Heart

Cancer has so much to give. Truly, he's got a heart of gold. He's also surprisingly outgoing and independent—and he's able to show the world what he's made of. In fact, he's definitely not the wallflower some astrologers make him out to be! He's a cardinal sign—meaning, of course, that he secretly likes to dominate. In other words, you won't find a Cancer bowing to another sign. He's regal. He knows how to turn things around to his advantage. Cancer has the world at his fingertips. How he chooses to use this awesome power depends on him.

Cancer's World

Cancers have incredible insight sometimes when dealing with the world. They know when to lay back and when to charge forward. Yes, they can be sly and manipulative (these traits, though, will disappear as they get older and learn). Eventually, they'll be able to somehow fit into society and adhere to its "strict" (to them) social demands.

At the same time, Cancers don't really like to march to the beat of the same drum as others. Though they're not as radical as Aquarians, they do like to go against the grain. Strangely enough, however, while Aquarians search out a mate who definitely can't be pegged into any one category, Cancers want someone who will meet with the appreciation and approval of his family. Real respect from a Cancer is very hard to come by. It may seem as if he's made you his world, but unless he also wants to make you part of his family, you've got nothing coming.

Maintaining Balance

Here's the key to a happy Cancer life: a regime that lets him be social when he feels like it and also to stay home and hide when he wants. Don't be fooled by gregarious Cancer. He likes his digs just as much or more than he likes the "out" life.

🅴❗ Alert

If a Cancer man or woman is stalling to get married, it probably means that it won't happen (it still can, but it's more unlikely). Cancer, when he finds the one for him, will balk and stall a little (even test the relationship by "messing up" once, perhaps) but, after that, he won't hesitate to procure a ring and rush to the altar. He needs to know his future is set and happily secure.

Cordial Cancer

Cancers are almost always cordial. They know how to deal with different types of people and how to make them feel comfortable and included. When they're out and about, they can come off as Fire signs because they're very good at striking up a conversation. They're also quite sexy and charismatic, and they have an exceptional flair for putting outfits together to show off their best assets.

🅴✳ Essential

Cancer will not give unsolicited information. If, however, you get specific instructions or advice, you should pay attention. Cancer is able to look at the big picture and get an intuition of what's going on—things you wouldn't normally notice.

Cancers are also great empathizers. They'll rarely pity someone for bad fortune—Cancer believes you should take charge of the situation and deal with it. But they have two strong, genuine shoulders to rely on if you're sick. One thing you may notice about Cancer is that he'll tell you what he thinks, but he'll rarely lecture you. Instead, he'll simply say the way things are, according to him. If you've done something wrong, Cancer will be the first to tell you what to do—but only if you ask for advice.

A Fine Romance

Somehow, you always get the feeling that Cancer is giving you compliments simply for the sake of it. You feel special for the moment until, suddenly, the flattery is being handed to the person next to you. How does she manage to always get away with it? Sometimes Cancer doesn't realize that people can see through the image she's created for herself—though this is of no concern. Cancer is projecting: hoping the compliments will fly back her way, too.

Family and Friends

It is also said that family life and home are both very important to Cancers. This is indubitably true. All Cancers are, in some way, tied to family—whether it's their own (husband, wife, children) or immediate (parents, siblings). Marriage and children are essential to most Cancers, and security in having this is one of Cancer's ultimate goals.

All Cancers are nurturing, especially the Cancer woman, who is sexy and always has some kind of feminine quality. This especially comes out with friends. She's like a mother hen, curious about gossip of new loves. In fact, she'll be a little offended if her friends don't keep her up to date on their families, too. The Cancer woman absolutely has to know what's going on and usually asks about your mom or your love life. In other words, the Cancer woman loves having other "in love" couples to hang out with.

The Art of Attraction

Most Cancers tend to see the world through rose-colored glasses. Although they can see many things in life clearly, love doesn't happen to be one of them. This doesn't stop Cancer, however. Unlike many people, he usually finds what he's looking for in a partner. Being wildly swept away is extremely important to Cancer. He wants the romance of a lifetime and usually gets it.

Once Cancer is in love, he tends to stay in love. He's good at keeping his mate—he knows just how to give her what she needs. Once he sees what he wants, he grabs on. He feels, therefore he is. However, if he's jilted, it may also take him a long time to let go.

The Long Haul

Needless to say, Cancer makes a wonderful love partner and parent. He dotes on everyone, and he's affectionate. He might even cook up a storm. He has lots of interesting friends from all walks of life. In a mate, he looks for security, both emotionally and financially (though his feelings of the heart will always win out over stock holdings). He also wants a woman whom he can greatly respect—one he'll be proud to call his. And he'll look for an ego booster in a wife: The Cancer man can be terribly insecure in private.

Cancers, early on in life, can have many flings and adventures. They're often curious and experimental—they like to try it all out. A less evolved Cancer may settle down too soon for fear of being alone. More mature Cancers usually wait for "The One" and live very happy, fulfilled lives. Many times Cancer can be quite faithful (Cancer men are less so), though if he feels he's not with his future wife, he won't think twice about cheating or dating two, even three other women at once.

e! Alert

A mature Cancer will find his place in the world and know just how to cope with happenings around him. A less evolved Cancer, though, will try to make the world adapt to him—all the while incorporating sneaky, deceptive maneuvers in order to "help" things get into place. An even less evolved Cancer will be like Dr. Jekyll and Mr. Hyde: sweet, sweet—then suddenly nasty. Choose wisely.

The Little Stuff Counts

The Cancer woman is impressed with worldly men, but she also likes her men to be simple in some way. She's attracted to men who calm her and who are generally tranquil—yet make her smile. She'll go for a man who looks great in jeans but who also cleans up well at a moment's notice. She likes a man who's sexy from the inside out: one who's discreet, not a poser, and certainly regal in bearing (in her mind).

The Cancer man also goes for sexy. Secretly, or for short periods of time, he may have relations with women who dress a little more on the suggestive side (or dally on the dark side, perhaps). Though he doesn't always admit it, the Cancer man likes to be shocked and challenged. However, this is not usually the woman he chooses to marry. The woman who is to be the Cancer man's partner for life will almost certainly be the one he can take home and present to Mama—a "good girl"—sweet, open, and one who will stand up to him when he does something wrong.

Pillow Talk: Signs in the Bedroom

A Cancer will never directly say she wants to go to bed. She'll hint and maybe even joke about it, but then she'll claim she was just kidding—even when she wasn't. If she's joking about it with you, chances are, she'd jump at the chance if offered to her. Most likely, she'll just go for it, physically. Cancers like sex—or rather, they like passionate sex.

The Secret Cancer Man

The Cancer man is a little confusing. He flirts continuously, never seeming to get enough of women: In fact, he doesn't know what he wants. But in truth, when the Cancer man gets hold of his moods and grows up, he can be a wonderful mate. He's a great lover: attentive and sexual. If you want to have a fling with him, keep in mind that it may be very short-lived. He'll show you all the attention in the world and make you feel like a goddess, but he probably won't call again. More likely, he'll show up at your door when he's been jilted by some current main squeeze. And once his self-confidence returns, he'll disappear again.

 Question

> **What's the one sure way to get a Crab man into bed?**
> Grab him. The Cancer man will happily let himself be seduced by an aggressive woman. If he's unsure or daw-dling about, the direct approach will work with him. Don't bother with words; just show him what you want with action.

The Secret Cancer Woman

Let the Cancer woman talk and show her that you really understand her. She's looking for a connection—however flimsy.

She'll fill in the gaps. She tends to go for a he-man, whether that means macho, sexy, dominant, or noble. She's pretty flexible on dates. Though she can dress to the nines, she'd also be up for a hayride or a water amusement park, for example. Cancer also loves to just hang out in front of the television.

Almost all Cancer women are also open-minded and perhaps New Age–oriented in some way. Seduce her by showing her you like the same spiritual books she likes or that you at least appreciate what she's interested in. She'll like you more for it. The Cancer woman can be touchy-feely if she's very into you, but she needs to feel comfortable before she starts getting intimate.

Sun Love Matches

Once again, Cancer can be idealistic. She's looking for the white picket fence and all the trimmings—a perfect husband, father, lover, cook, and domestic live-in who will always be affectionate with her. Cancer simply doesn't like to fight. If she's involved with a person with many planets in Fire, she may choose to run (which is a shame—both have fierce defense mechanisms. If they stay, they'll eventually get along amazingly well). Also, she feels her way through the world, so an Air sign, or someone who rationalizes too much and bursts her idealistic bubble, will not likely be the one to capture her heart. Read on to learn about the love compatibility pairs with the female Crab.

Cancer Man

These two are both romantic, and they know how to give each other the emotional support each craves. Though they tend to be possessive with each other, the problems that mount seem to cancel one another out. In other words, these two mix well, though dangerously. In bed, they have the same style, though both secretly would like to dominate. To others, they appear to be soul mates. If one of the two doesn't have too much Air or Earth, this can be a very passionate, dramatic relationship. Should they find a way to be honest and to trust each other deeply, this can be a possible long-term relationship, with an okay chance for marriage. However, the moodiness of the two together? One is high tide, one may be low; and how do you control the waves of an ocean?

Leo Man

No other sign in the zodiac knows how to give a good compliment like the Cancer woman—and the Leo man just eats this up. She's deep and emotional, and he finds that strangely affecting. She understands him and lets him know it. She talks more than he does and opens him up like a sunflower. But he's actually not sure if he can trust her fully. He doesn't quite get why she pulls back from him—and when she does, he does it, too. This can be confusing to both. But when the Leo man gets insecure about the relationship, Cancer knows just how to come back and make him feel good again. In bed, the Leo man is able to open Cancer up and make her purr. This can be a possible long-term partnership and an excellent marriage (one of the best) . . . especially if the Leo man steps aside and lets the Cancer woman take the lead.

 **Essential**

Cancer and Leo can bring out the best in each other, as long as Cancer is honest about her feelings without getting too emotional. This way, Leo can trust her observations and honor them.

Virgo Man

The Cancer woman tolerates the Virgo man to a point. But she wants more romance from him—more candlelight, more music, and a clearer demonstration of feelings. She knows he's crazy about her. Why doesn't he show it more? And why does he have to analyze every point? In fact, he repeats himself. Cancer gets the feeling he does it just to hear himself talk. Though she's able to soothe his ego, she sometimes gets annoyed when he's critical or judgmental, and at these times she's not likely to feel like giving him that extra attention. However, Virgo's smitten. The Cancer woman wishes he'd put her before his work. Cancer and Virgo both like sex, and she sometimes wonders if Virgo is really in the moment or somewhere else. If Virgo can open up to the Cancer woman, this can be a possible long-term relationship and a possible marriage, though not a recommended one unless both can't imagine a life without the other and are determined to make it work.

Libra Man

When they actually get around to talking about the rapport they have together, Libra and Cancer find they have a lot in common. Unfortunately, the two keep beating around the bush, and the problems can mount when they're both purposely avoiding confrontation. Cancer senses when Libra is unhappy, and the two really affect each other, producing strange and powerful up-and-down mood swings. Instinctively, the Cancer woman knows how to stroke Libra's libido. He sees her as the perfect woman and mother figure. In bed, Libra may seem a bit distant for Cancer. One day, Libra is a passionate whirlwind; the next he's as cold as an iceberg. Cancer wishes she could repair the sometimes-dark side of Libra's soul and make him think more idealistically and less rationally. This can be a possible long-term relationship, but it is not a probable marriage . . . unless the Libra man is willing to stick it out when things get tough and can respond to Cancer's dreams.

☑ Fact

Cancers have incredible influence over the general public. How they choose to use this power is up to them. Famous Crabs with this kind of charisma include Princess Diana, the Dalai Lama, P. T. Barnum, Ross Perot, Nancy Reagan, Frida Kahlo, and John Quincy Adams.

Scorpio Man

This can be a very good combination for the Cancer woman. If she can overlook his political views and deal with his periods of stress from too much work (or lack thereof), the two can be a match made in heaven. Sexually, dark Scorpio will subtly convince Cancer to take charge. She'll do it with gusto, and the two of them in bed find exactly what they're looking for. These two are also incredibly dramatic. Scorpio wants Cancer to prove she's trustworthy. Cancer is able to do that once she sees she can trust him. Cancer is funny, smart, and never predictable—which will thrill Scorpio to the hilt. This is a probable long-term relationship with an excellent chance for marriage as well . . . as long as Scorpio doesn't rain all over Cancer's parade.

Sagittarius Man

This is a classic case of opposites that really do attract. The Sagittarius man is very different from the Cancer woman, yet they seem to be good for each other at times. In fact, the Sagittarius man is able to give the Cancer woman a good boost of energetic power. She'll love the outings and adventures he takes her on. She's fascinated and warmed by the fact that he's so good at everything he does. And Sagittarius thinks the Cancer woman is great; he respects her. The right words and silences Cancer offers him make him love and appreciate her more. She probably wishes he'd open up more to her. In bed, the Cancer woman finds a sexual partner who can please her and make her feel loved. If Sagittarius can be faithful (he will be—only for "The One") and let the Cancer woman rule his domain, this can be a very possible long-term relationship with a good chance for marriage. The question is: Will she tolerate his caveman approach to love?

e✔ Fact

When you think of Sagittarius men, think "different." Woody Allen, Mark Twain, Steven Spielberg, Beethoven, and Walt Disney are all good examples of the Archer's famous, brilliant imagination.

Capricorn Man

The Cancer woman may find the Capricorn man a stickler for so many things. Why can't he loosen up a little? In truth, either the two will see life completely through rose-colored glasses, or Capricorn will simply burst Cancer's romantic, visionary bubble (depending on Capricorn's chart). Thank goodness he's faithful. Cancer loves this about him and that he can be a rock for her—one she knows she can always lean on. Unfortunately, bed and sexuality may be a bit of a problem. Capricorn can be more practical than Cancer—in many ways. If he can open up a little, he may just be able to tap into her hidden sensual, sexual energies. If Capricorn can learn to lighten up, these two can find a possible long-term relationship together. Still, they are not a probable marriage unless Cancer seeks assurance and stability with a he-man sort—the kind who will not let her run things. Some female Cancers are okay with that . . . but only about 5 percent.

Aquarius Man

The Cancer woman is intrigued by the Aquarius man. He's sexy, and he's out there. Together, these two can become wanderlust bohemians. He brings out her spiritual side. They're also both incredibly intuitive. However, both can be deceptively blocked—especially the Cancer woman when she wants to be. This bothers Aquarius, who sees himself as straightforward. Then again, he's able to wait out Cancer's push-pull techniques. Aquarius, in bed, likes it rougher than Cancer. Instead, she wonders if he's able to stay with her and only her. These two excite each other mentally, though, and can really talk through the night. This could be a possible long-term relationship, and a possible marriage beyond that, although Aquarius's dark side (he safely protects) will eventually come out and may even scare her into running. These two should take a long time getting to know each other before tying the knot.

Pisces Man

The Pisces man intrigues the Cancer woman. She has all the time in the world to get to know him and will give her best effort in doing so. Romantically and emotionally, the Fish is perfect for the Crab. The only problem here can be with "push-pull" on both parts—when angry, she crawls and he swims away. Also, the Pisces man may or may not be the financial breadwinner Cancer hopes for, and he can sometimes be a downer with his weight-of-the-world reality views. However, this doesn't always turn Cancer away. She is still wowed by Pisces's intuition and creativity. Soft, slow, romantic, and passionate sex heats up the rapport in bed. If Pisces can give in to Cancer's nurturing instinct, this can be a probable long-term relationship with an excellent chance for marriage—just bear in mind that Pisces will get more of the "me" time of the two water signs. Yes, much to Cancer's dismay, Pisces definitely can take hold as the central being here more aptly if he wants.

e✱ Essential

Many Cancer women and Pisces men see things the same way in terms of family and can work well together to create a perfect home atmosphere. Probably, both want children.

Aries Man

The Aries man conquers Cancer's heart. He woos her, makes her feel special, and spoils her. Predictably, she gets hooked on the Ram. Even when he begins looking around at others, she tries to turn a blind eye to his flirtatious side, hoping it's just his way. In bed, he knows how to tap into her creative energies. Lovemaking becomes a wild ride for both of them—adventurous, passionate, and even a little kinky. The Aries man also loves when Cancer dotes on him. If she's strong enough to let him wander off with friends into his social habitat, he'll always come back to her. But this takes a lot of willpower for the Cancer woman. If she can do it, this can be a possible long-term relationship, with marriage possible . . . but only if Cancer if willing to concede that Aries is always right (even when he's not).

Taurus Man

With Taurus, Cancer knows she'll be taken care of. She relies on him and likes the feeling of security he gives her. She doesn't expect him to be unfaithful—and, most likely, he won't be—but Taurus falls in love with his head first, and Cancer with her heart. Cancer is much wiser than Taurus when it comes to judgment of people. Even so, he absolutely won't listen to her advice, and it gets him into a lot of trouble. In bed, Taurus has all the sensual moves Cancer craves. However, she may be a bit shy with him in the beginning—he wishes she'd just tell him what she wants. If the two can let go of emotional doubts and fears of the past, this can be a possible long-term relationship. It's also a possible marriage, though not a likely one, unless Taurus has been through a lot and can be reflective, generous, and moralistic in Cancer's eyes.

Gemini Man

Both are open-minded, curious, and outgoing. Though this is always true of Gemini, Cancer is only bubbly when she feels like it. Many times, in fact, Cancer would prefer a quiet candlelit dinner at home, while Gemini has other plans. He wants to go out and show off his lady love to others. Also, Gemini tells fibs here and there. Cancer, though, knows just how to play him right—if there's anyone who can get him to confess, it's the Crab. Creatively, these two spur each other on. In bed, their styles vary greatly, and Gemini would prefer to go faster and change positions more frequently. To Cancer, this starts to feel like sexual gymnastics—all the moves and none of the emotions. If the Gemini man has some Fire or a lot of Water in his chart, this combo may work. If not, this is a possible long-term relationship but not a probable marriage . . . although there will be tons of drama and bonding figuring out what's best for them—either way.

 **Question**

> **Both Geminis and Cancers are instinctive. What's the difference?**
> Geminis are instinctive when it comes to words: giving a pep talk to a friend, for example. Cancers, instead, can intuit how a person is feeling—and usually react accordingly. They give space when it's warranted and hugs when needed.

Love Planets: Venus and Mercury

Cancer in anyone's chart—even those with mostly all Fire or all Air, for example—will always enjoy dinners at home and long for a nice family life. Though his other signs may fight with this part of him, romantic notions will always creep into the psyche of a person with Cancer influence. Below are the side effects you can expect with Cancer in your personal chart.

Venus in Cancer

Even if you have Air and Fire throughout your chart, Venus in Cancer will always make you a bit idealistic in love . . . okay, obsessed sometimes. You long for romance, and you dream of being swept away by passion and desire. Venus in Cancer is also the hardest aspect to have if you want to let go of a relationship gone wrong. A mate perfect for you would have to match your main influences. If you're mostly Water, look for the same in other people. Venus in Cancer can also conflict with your other signs. For instance, if you're a Leo or an Aries, this Cancer aspect will fight with your need to travel and be out and about. You'll find that, later on in life, your need for stability will win out and you'll settle down and get comfortable.

Venus in Cancer pairs well with Venus in Scorpio, Aries, Leo, and Cancer.

Mercury in Cancer

You're great at giving advice, but you wish people would listen to what you're saying. Because you're not as pushy as Leo (also a great advice giver), others don't take in and reflect on your words of wisdom as much as they should. You're instinctive and know how to get confessions out of people—making them talk about things they wouldn't normally. You sincerely care about people and are uncannily adept at giving the perfect compliment. Mercury in Cancer goes well with Mercury in Pisces, Scorpio, Cancer, and Leo.

CHAPTER 5

Leo

Leo has so much presence that he lights up a room and forces everyone to look his way. He also has the sunniest disposition of all the signs of the zodiac . . . when he feels like it. Just remember that lions occasionally do roar. And when he does, it's best to get out of his way. In this chapter, find out what makes Leo the powerful, dramatic soul he is.

Can You Turn a Fierce Lion into a Pussycat?

1. **Which would Leo consider to be not only annoying but also a deal breaker?**
   A. Loquaciousness
   B. Arrogance
   C. Vanity
   D. Pettiness

2. **What's the best way to handle a Leo man who has just insulted you?**
   A. Laugh it off; no big deal.
   B. Insult him back—an eye for an eye.
   C. Tell him he's totally inappropriate (in a sharp tone).
   D. Cry. Tears always work.

3. **If you were to take Leo away on vacation in the winter to simply relax, which place would be ideal?**
   A. A secluded camping ground with a tent for the two of you
   B. Someplace in Europe with charming little sidewalk cafes
   C. A mountain lodge with skiing and restaurants
   D. A beautiful beach resort with dancing and a casino

4. **Which is not one of Leo's traits?**
   A. Cockiness
   B. Loyalty
   C. Insincerity
   D. Generosity

5. **The Leo woman wants a man, above all, whom she can:**
   A. Tell what to do
   B. Learn from
   C. Teach
   D. Shape

6. **If Leo were brought to a party, knowing no one, Leo would:**
   A. Hide in the corner
   B. Find one person to talk with
   C. Search for the person Leo came with originally
   D. Make friends with everyone

7. **How does the typical Leo feel about "The One"?**
   A. Exists, for sure
   B. Doesn't exist
   C. Never wanted it
   D. Couldn't care less

8. **You've just had a small fight with a Leo mate. What do you do?**
   A. Make him see your side
   B. Beg for forgiveness
   C. Tell him you see his side—and then actually try to see it
   D. Leave him alone and wait for him to come to you

9. **How does Leo flirt—most of the time?**
   A. Through words
   B. Through body language

10. **How does Leo feel about coarse language in bed?**
    A. Doesn't usually belong there
    B. Nasty is good
    C. The more, the better
    D. Depends on the position, the time, the place, and the person

The Generous Lion

There's almost no one as generous as Leo the Lion. In fact, she's much more comfortable with giving than getting. The Lion will also spend when she has the chance, buying gifts for herself and for others without waiting for a holiday or any specific reason. Returning the favor with a gift will be nice for Leo, and she'll probably adore you for it. However, the one thing she wants more than anything is your appreciation and devotion. She needs to be respected and admired. In fact, she'll gravitate toward you if you can give her this without ceremony.

 Fact

In love, Leo wants someone as giving as she is. This is where many astrologers get it wrong. Financial gifts work up to a point, it's true, but Leo looks for an emotional connection more than anything. She longs to be persuaded and to be treated like she's the only woman on earth.

Though Leo is all Fire, she feels deeply. She instinctively knows who really cares about her and who doesn't—though she tends to project her feelings on others at times. This means that if she doesn't like someone, she'll immediately think the person doesn't like her either. No matter—Leo goes by a sense of skin. If a person rubs her the wrong way, she'll simply turn away and reject the friendship or love situation. Once you've gotten on the bad side of Leo, too, there's not much you can do to win her over again. She'll forgive you, but she'll never forget.

Queenly/Kingly Behavior

Like Pisces, Leo always has a sophisticated air about him. He can rise from humble beginnings, but he'll always find a way to come out on top. He's regal and, some believe, even pretentious (if they don't know him). His nature is real; his judgment is off until he matures and centers himself. Also, Leo doesn't particularly like to conform. He'll try a situation out, but if it's not to his liking, he won't hesitate to quickly move away from it.

🔔 **Alert**

Leo can be your best friend or love mate. Though he's never out to hurt anyone, he'll talk behind your back or betray you if he believes you're not real with him! With Leo it's all or nothing: You're either with him or against him.

Even so, Leo is the best friend you can have. If he's a real friend, he'll be completely devoted to you. He'll keep all your secrets. He'll shower you with attention and affection. He'll be your champion in love. Although he's faithful, he won't be true to you for one minute if he thinks you're full of it.

The Art of Attraction

Leo will always root for the underdog. She deeply empathizes with the one she believes to be in the right and will fight tooth and nail for him (like Aquarius, except that Leo is less naive). She always assesses the situation first and then takes action. Sometimes she can be apathetic, but if the person is a true friend, she'll do everything she can to help.

Above all, Leo despises pettiness in others. Signs of the zodiac who pick a fight for no reason or who have some of these traits will never win a Leo's heart. Leo is always a noble creature, and she expects those around her to be as well.

The Long Haul

Pride is a genuine factor when considering a Leo as a future mate. Ego is essential to a Lion. Many think that Leo is cocky and full of herself, but this isn't usually so. Instead, Leo is insecure and worries that people won't recognize her as powerful. In fact, keeping a Lion happy almost always has to do with stroking her ego the right way. If she's constantly made jealous or treated badly, she'll keep with the relationship only to see if she can turn things around. Leo's an optimist at heart, and sometimes her ego steers her will, too. But if she can't take the heat any longer, she'll sprint off to find cooler waters.

 Fact

Leos let pride determine who their partner will be. They want someone who's faithful and loving, who will tell them how wonderful they are at all times. An insecure Leo is not a pretty sight.

However, Leo can't stand those who fawn all over her. She wants a partner with a real spine who can stand up to her and take control. Yes, Leo is strong—in some ways. You'd think she wanted a mate to carry out her every whim. Not so. She does want someone who will go along with her, but she also needs a partner who will put her in her place if need be, someone who has good judgment. More than anything, Leo needs to respect a partner intensely. Without the grand respect, Leo can fall into lust, but never in love.

The Little Stuff Counts

To lose a Leo fast, dress scruffily or show up at her doorstep unkempt. Leo will take you to a little hole in the wall because she doesn't want to be seen with you. Appearance is important to Leo, whether man or woman. Leo takes great care in dressing for a date, and she expects you to do the same. Hair is very important to Leos. For a Leo man, a woman with long, beautiful hair is a fantastic turn-on. Compliment a Leo woman on her eyes, and she'll be yours for the evening.

Leo always goes for sexy. A man with an earring won't turn a Leo woman off—if it's tasteful. However, she will find excessive jewelry on a man to be too much. Contrary to popular belief, Leo does not like ostentatious showoffs. The male Lion goes for sexy and subtle. Remember, too, that Leo likes to feel she's won someone over with her charm and intelligence. If Leo's date starts checking out other girls while she's on his arm, she'll play it cool, but she'll also take away all Brownie points. Again, you won't win by making Leo angry.

🅴 Alert

> Though Leo can hold her own in any verbal war, she'll blame you for making her lose her cool. She doesn't like to fight and won't stay long with a partner who reduces her to it.

Though Leo doesn't like to fight, she does like challenge. If she wins a partner too easily, she'll wonder why. Cocky as she may seem, though, she'll never think, "Oh, I conquered him right away because I'm wonderful." Cancer might think this, but Leo won't. Also remember that Leo goes by feeling and instinct more than by rationalization. She's all Fire and wants to be swept away with love and desire.

Pillow Talk: Signs in the Bedroom

Leo is lusty and loves sex. Leo longs to be won over, body and soul. A little playfulness in the bedroom helps the Lion feel more relaxed. Like a cat, people of this sign can be curious, too, about all kinds of bed play. Though he'll shy away from sex toys—perhaps indicating to you that he thinks they're vulgar—this may be all for show. Secretly, he'll hope you can find just the right way to persuade him into trying them.

 **Essential**

Leo is a romantic at heart and must decide beforehand if a partner is just a sex mate or a long-term relationship. He's capable, though, of having a fling if he's convinced it won't hurt anyone—especially himself.

The Secret Leo Man

It has been said that Leos are not as strong and sturdy as they seem. This is sometimes doubly true of the male Lion. Always remember that narcissism is a product of deep insecurity. He appears to be sleek, cool, and graceful. He speaks through movements rather than through words—a smile, a shake of the head, a wink, or a touch—body language. If he talks a lot, he's covering a silence that, to him, is unbearable. Leo men are notoriously critical of themselves.

Sarcastic Barbs

Both Sagittarius and Leo men (also Cancer and Scorpio, depending) are known for their sarcastic barbs. If it's teasing, fine. Tease back. But their subtle yet rude comments are designed to put you off guard and off balance. This comes from a need to see what you're made of, to test if you can stand up to them, and, quite possibly, to reduce others. You see, this is the ruse they sometimes use to feel better about themselves and to distract the conversation back to you, away from them. Can you handle it? (They want to know.) Your only good counter against this is to reply with a mature, noble answer. If you use sarcasm or nastiness back, ironically enough, Leo will feel like you're the one attacking him.

 Fact

A more evolved Leo won't use sarcasm to belittle you. If you know a Leo who does, don't reduce yourself to his level. He won't respect you for it. Instead, give him an ultimatum. If he feels he'll lose you because of his insensitivity, he'll quickly change his ways.

The King of the Bedroom

One important thing to remember is that the Leo man absolutely must dominate in bed. If you're aggressive with him, he won't like it. He needs to feel like a real he-man. This is essential to him. In fact, if you're a little reluctant with him at first, it works just fine. He needs to believe you are "swept away" by his efforts. Sexually, the Leo man also needs to feel loved and nurtured. He likes being "mommied." He runs hot and cold, though. If he feels he loves you in the moment, he's a dynamo who will put the biggest player's romantic repertoire to shame. If he doesn't, you may just feel like a tornado has hit you and left you with no possessions. When he's truly in it for the long haul, though, he'll never waiver with his affections.

A Sensitive Soul

The Leo man is sensitive, too. If you insult him about his lovemaking, he won't defend himself and try to make it better (the way Aries would). And he certainly won't let it roll off his back easily (as Sagittarius does). Instead, he'll instinctively get a bad feeling about you without consciously knowing where it came from. He'll push you away. Then he'll look elsewhere for a partner who makes him feel good about himself.

The Secret Leo Woman

She also appears strong, but she has barriers up. Deep down, she doesn't realize that she has awesome power. Once she taps into this, it's smooth sailing. Again, a Leo woman can be insecure, too. Her need for compliments is unusually insatiable. But they better be real or Leo will sense it. Unlike a Leo man, a Leo woman needs to be dominated completely. Read that again. She's good at being aggressive and taking charge in bed, but she doesn't really like it. Instead, she wants deep, powerful, mysterious sex. Sex is the only place she's convinced herself that she can let down her guard.

 Alert

The Leo woman has constant scripts and scenarios running in her head. If you can say just the right words or touch her in just the right place, she'll be yours. She may even feel that your connection with her is destiny.

Leos, like Virgos, are very selective about their friends and mates. Virgo, though, will sometimes give more of a chance than Leo will—even though Virgo trusts less.

Oh, and here's one more thing: Don't ever try to manipulate a Leo woman, in or out of bed. The Leo woman may come off as a femme fatale, but that's because she chooses to be seen that way. It's a defense mechanism. She may like to play and provoke, but she's almost never sneaky or deceptive like Gemini or Scorpio. And she'll hate it if you think that she is. Instead, if a Leo woman is reserved and doesn't speak up about something that's bothering her, either ask her what's wrong or let it pass. Don't immediately assume that Leo is formulating some scheme against you. She isn't. Deep down, Leo's good. Treat her like the nobility she is, and you'll always win with the female Lion.

Sun Love Matches

The Leo woman always looks for a mate who excites her. She hates being bored (just like the Aries woman). In fact, she sometimes gets into trouble because she has a habit of going for dangerous, dark souls whom she believes she can rescue and bring to the light. In this way, she's attracted to Scorpio, Cancer, and Aries men—though these matches don't necessarily last. The Leo man, on the other hand, may want excitement, but he also intensely craves security and a mother figure. He wants a mate who he knows will take good care of his future brood. Only a mature Leo man will be faithful, but he will always expect it of his partner. Once again, jealousy is not the way to win any Leo's heart.

Keep in mind that the Leo man is not necessarily looking for the same things in a mate as the Leo woman. (See individual signs to learn more about pairings with the Leo man.) Read on to learn about love matches with the Leo woman.

e✔ Fact

Many Leo men, by the way, also have a hidden desire to have children born from love between him and "The One." This is just something he instinctively wishes for from childhood to maturity.

Leo Man

Many times, two signs together make a perfect match, but it's not necessarily so with two Leos. Male and female Lions require so much attention and adoration that satisfaction in this pairing is difficult. However, they get each other and speak the same language—that's good. It's an especially precarious balance to attain, though, for two people striving for the same goal. In bed, the Leo man's hot-and-cold streaks drive the Leo woman crazy—for good or for bad. This match purely depends on the type of Leo you're dealing with. If the two are mature, this can be a possible long-term relationship, even a possible marriage . . . but is the Leo woman strong enough to keep the Leo man in check? Sometimes, yes.

Virgo Man

This is, perhaps, an odd choice for a Leo woman. As a friend, though, these two go wonderfully together. They both like the finer things in life, and Virgo can be generous with the Leo woman. Leo also loves the way Virgo can judge people. Secretly, she does it, too. Though Virgo is a bit freer with his trust, he's able to find a good balance in naming friends and foes. In bed, however, Virgo doesn't normally open up enough for the Leo woman. Leo is also much more affectionate than

Virgo, in general. And when he gets nitpicky and starts dissecting situations and people, Leo goes insane. This man can be too mentally heavy for Leo, who wants excitement but also tranquillity. This is not necessarily the makings of a long-term relationship, and though it's not a likely marriage either, it's been done. However, Virgo usually feels like he's given his "all" while Leo usually feels like he hasn't given enough.

Libra Man

Like Leo, Libra loves beautiful settings. He fascinates the Leo woman. They're both trying to figure each other out. Leo doesn't necessarily trust Libra, but she loves his charm, his sexy ways, and his wit. Libra can be distant in bed, but when he's really there, the Leo woman is completely taken by him. It's just too bad that he thinks she wants to lead. Deep down, she hopes he'll rise up to the challenge and dominate her more. This is a possible long-term relationship, but it's not a probable marriage . . . though, again, if there's love there—who's to say?

🅔✔ Fact

Leo usually scares the Libra man too much to be a choice for a long-term mate. He sees her as a risk; a femme fatale out to break him. He keeps weighing the odds of being with her. He's sometimes critical with her, though she handles it well.

Scorpio Man

Leo's convinced she's not in love with him. Then, out of nowhere, she falls. How did that happen? Perhaps she was busy keeping up with his moods. His self-pity drives her crazy, but she loves the idea of rescuing him from his dark side. She loves all his mystery. In fact, if she had to pinpoint when she first had real feelings for him, she'll realize, most likely, it was when she finally went to bed with him. To her, he's a wonderful lover—sensual, sexual, and intense. In the bedroom, these two can be a match made in heaven. Out of the bedroom, however, they have all kinds of quarrels and misunderstandings. This is a very probable long-term relationship, but it's not a recommended marriage—although this really depends on Scorpio's chart . . . and how much Scorpio is willing to be dedicated to her. If "completely" is the answer, it can definitely work.

Sagittarius Man

There are two kinds of Sagittarius men—the dark, pensive kind who only talks when he has something to say (a caveman type) and the happy-go-lucky puppy-dog variety. Leo is attracted to the first kind. There's something dangerous about him. She fears she has to tiptoe around him and will walk a fine line to keep him from going off the deep end. She puts up with it, though. Why? He's one of the most intelligent men around. And interesting. Sexy. She respects him. He's adventurous, take-charge, and macho. He's one of the only men she'll allow to dominate her.

e! Alert

It's not common, but it happens sometimes: Sagittarius men can have a terrible temper. Like Gemini women, it's innate. Be careful! A Leo woman will sometimes tolerate emotional abuse but never physical . . . not even the hint of it.

And in the bedroom? Sag is a stallion! A Casanova! Incredible! He excites her like no one else (except maybe Scorpio). If Leo can control herself, and not get too aggressive or dramatic with the male Archer (who despises scenes, private or public), this can be a probable long-term relationship and a very possible marriage . . . double that if she's secure with herself and doesn't rile him up to the point where his respect dwindles.

Capricorn Man

The Capricorn man can sometimes be a bit "black or white" for the sunny Leo woman, who's more open in her outlook on life. But if he's not jaded and still has some of the wonder he's naturally born with, these two can play and laugh. She loves his ironic sense of humor. He also gives her a sense of security that she finds very attractive. Sometimes, though, he gets too close for comfort. He understands her (perhaps a little too much— or reads into things that sometimes aren't there), and this can spell trouble. He analyzes and criticizes her. She protects herself by pretending he doesn't have it right, though she knows deep down that he's right on the money (when he is). In bed, sparks don't fly the way she hopes. The Capricorn man holds back. He's got secrets and all kinds of issues, she thinks. She may or may not be correct in this assumption. If Capricorn can ease up a little, this can be a possible long-term partnership and a possible marriage beyond that . . . especially if they get their bedroom liaisons in order and communication on par.

Aquarius Man

In the beginning, Aquarius is so easy to be with. He's the male best friend she never had. She's amazed by his social skills and his natural ability to communicate and tell a good story. She thinks she's found "The One." But then the problems start. She gets annoyed and even jealous when all his buddies run to him when they need cheering up. And he always drops her to help them. Sexually, their partnership is wonderful, but she may feel there's something missing. She just can't put her finger on what that is. Aquarius thinks Leo is a bit too sensitive. Why can't she lighten up? If Aquarius uses his instincts more with Leo and is careful with her feelings, this can be a possible long-term relationship, even a possible marriage . . . although this pairing is more likely to happen later in life when the two are mature and can appreciate each other for who they really are.

Pisces Man

The Pisces man can get immediately obsessed with the Leo woman if he doesn't conquer her fully. She loves the look in his eyes and his deep analyses of the people around them. Pisces also adores Leo's sense of humor and her zest for life. His little comments and compendium of strange facts make her laugh. If Leo has one or two Water signs in her chart, Pisces can be good for her. He actually brings out the best in her at times. He knows just how to play her and can cheer her up on a moment's notice. Problem is, he can also bring her down when he feels like it, too. It's like that.

Though Pisces can be a trustworthy soul, Leo sometimes doesn't know what to make of him. She needs to know him better before she can trust him. Once she does, she sees that he is definitely worthy of her. Pisces, too, is able to adjust to his surroundings the same way Leo can. He's got an innate sense of refinement and style. She just wishes he would stop pulling away, getting quiet when things get tough. She takes charge, which she despises in many situations. Deep down, she wants her man to know what to do in any situation and when to do it: to be her hero. If Leo doesn't feel that Pisces manipulates her too much, this can be a probable long-term relationship and even a possible marriage. Leo just better make sure that she is "The One and Only" for him before accepting the ring.

Aries Man

The Aries man gets Leo excited, and she wonders where he gets all his energy. In the beginning, it seems as if they really "get" each other. They admire each other's sense of style and way of handling things. Aries also inspires Leo's creativity, and a compliment from him goes a long way for the Lioness. However, Aries's attention is sometimes over the top and then changes to sporadic, at best. It depends on how mature he is. Leo will follow him around for a while, but then she'll want to retreat into her cave—Aries will want to follow. If she lets him in, he can woo her easily. In bed, they can be a great match. Thank goodness Aries is a real man, she thinks. She also loves the fact that people look up to him. Together they know how to paint the town. If Aries remains interested in her and doesn't hurt Leo's hypersensitive ego, this couple can be a long-term relationship. They may even make for an excellent marriage. Again, this depends on Aries—and whether he's mature enough to make Leo happy, whatever it takes. However, Leo may tire of the Aries man's unwarranted arrogance. This may just be a case of "too much of a good thing" at first—that may sadly burn out (Aries dives headfirst). That's not Leo's fault.

Taurus Man

He seems almost like a Fire sign when she first meets him. He's charming and possibly even a bit dangerous. Leo's definitely attracted to him. There's one big problem: Taurus can be petty. He doesn't like the way she spends money. She doesn't like the way he's generous for things that apply only to him. Either he lectures her incessantly about her financial status, or he keeps quiet and withdraws from her without explaining why. He also makes her jealous by flirting with her friends. In bed, think heat, sensuality, passion, and intensity. He's got a nice style for her—he can dominate her completely and still service her in all the ways she wants. He won't stop until she's satiated. This can be an excellent long-term affair, but it is not a recommended marriage; however, many couples have done it successfully. It would just take tons of work.

ⓔ✱ Essential

Taurus is old-fashioned. He wants to control the Lioness by telling her how she should act. It bothers him that she's so outgoing and nice to people when he wants her just for himself.

Gemini Man

The Leo woman thinks that the Gemini man has commitment issues (he does—think "Peter Pan: I won't grow up"). But Leo can't help herself. Gemini not only has a magnetic sense of innate sexiness but also makes her laugh and lighten up. He's street-smart, and she respects this about him. He's kind. He knows how to deal with things (out of the box) in a way she could never dream of, and he's especially great with kids. He's approachable, and she feels comfortable with him. In fact, she loves spending alone time with him: Too bad he always has fans waiting on the sidelines. Thank goodness the Gemini man doesn't fight dirty like his female counterpart can. The Gemini man thinks the Lioness is all woman and tries to show her so in bed. Leo, though, gets the feeling that sex is a sport to Gemini (leg here, arm there; switch). Leo likes to be more spontaneous: less talking. If Gemini has some Fire or Water in his chart, this can be a possible long-term relationship. If so, it's a possible marriage . . . but both must really feel it in their hearts.

Cancer Man

These two connect in some strange way. The Cancer man brings out Leo's nurturing instincts, and he's able to take care of her in return. Although the two make an odd match, their relationship can work in and out of the bedroom. She gets hooked on his ups and downs, which can be exciting for her in a way that's not necessarily healthy.

 Fact

The Cancer man knows just the right thing to say to the Leo woman and when to say it. She respects him, though she's not sure if she should trust him. If he's sneaky or manipulative with her, unfortunately, she may just get addicted to the wrong guy.

When making love, these two can get adventurous together, and Cancer makes Leo feel things she didn't know she could. If Cancer is evolved, this can be a positive long-term relationship, and a very possible marriage beyond that. Again, Cancer must be a grownup—and Leo must be strong enough to call him on his antics.

Love Planets: Venus and Mercury

Leo is sunny, outgoing, protective, funny, and cool. Having a little Leo in your other planets is always a plus, with many more positive side effects than negative. First, check out your sign in Venus and Mercury. Then read on. Leo also always adds a little luck to anyone's life. Leos are unusually blessed with good fortune.

Venus in Leo

A grand love is your absolute ideal. You like everything grand. In fact, big, sweet gestures and romantic moves thrill you. Though you may have suffered earlier on in life, you tend to be an optimist at heart. You either trust or you don't. When you do, you can be faithful and loyal to a fault. You're attracted to people who seem to need you. You like to be in control, but you want someone who can also dominate you or you won't fall in love. If you are a woman with Venus in Leo, you love sex and long to be completely seduced. A man with Venus in Leo wants to feel deeply but fears he won't. You go well with Venus in Leo, Scorpio, Cancer, Sagittarius, and Aries.

Mercury in Leo

There is nothing that frustrates you more than a person who talks around and around the point without actually getting to it. It drives you nuts. You'll find some good excuse and be out the door before the talker can realize what's happened. You mean what you say, and you're good at grasping the situation for what it really is, but you tend to be idealistic—you wish everyone would follow through on their claims and promises (the way you always do). You forgive easily but never forget. You have a talent for recognizing and accepting people for who they are. People also like talking with you, and they think you're pretty cool and crafty. Mercury in Leo goes well with Mercury in Aquarius, Cancer, Leo, Aries, and Sagittarius.

CHAPTER 6

Virgo

Sometimes you can predict what Virgo may do, but other times he'll surprise you. Many Virgos are born with built-in protective walls. They only let you see what they want you to see. Here, discover what's going on behind the tricky Virgo façade that goes something like, "I'm fine, you're fine, now leave me alone . . . Wait! Where are you going?"

Are You Ready for the Noble Virgo?

1. **What is one thing that may be true about Virgo's sense of humor?**
   A. It's a little corny.
   B. It's on the "old-soul" side.
   C. It's very "in your face."
   D. It's a bit offbeat, maybe a little twisted.

2. **What's the best description of Virgo's preferred style of dating?**
   A. A Player: They date frequently.
   B. A Bad Boy or Girl: They're out to cause trouble.
   C. A Serial Monogamist: They usually have one serious relationship after the next.
   D. Shy: They wait for the other sex to come to them.

3. **True or False: Virgo will stay in a bad relationship for a long time, believing she can make it work.**
   A. True
   B. False

4. **What is a typical Virgo male downfall when it comes to picking a mate?**
   A. They're dominators—they need to be in charge.
   B. They're rescuers—they look to save and get hooked.
   C. They're morally corrupt—they don't always do the right thing.
   D. They're needy—they want constant attention.

5. **Which of the following Virgo celebrities has not been linked with a sex scandal?**
   A. Hugh Grant
   B. Charlie Sheen
   C. Kobe Bryant
   D. Adam Sandler

6. What may be a big turnoff for Virgo woman?

A. Telling her you like a certain position in bed

B. Asking for her help when you need it

C. Talking directly with her

D. Being possessive with her

7. If the two of you are getting along and Virgo suddenly uses sarcasm, it's usually meant to be:

A. Mean

B. Teasing

C. Confrontational

D. A power play

8. How is Virgo with money?

A. Cheap with it

B. Methodical about it

C. Spendthrift

D. Doesn't worry about it

9. What will really win over Virgo's heart? Someone who.

A. Makes him think

B. Makes him laugh out loud

C. Analyzes him well

D. Is not afraid to boss him around

10. True or False: Virgos believe people are either with them or against them.

A. True

B. False

The Selective One

Virgo can shut himself off from the world, but most of the time he seems outgoing and friendly. Though his quick, funny comebacks aren't meant to hurt, these comments can sometimes be sarcastic or biting. Don't read too much into it. Virgo is more likely to mock himself than to put the joke on you. In fact, a Virgo's worst enemy is usually himself. He has to be especially careful to treat himself well and not to wander down the path of self-pity. True, he bounces back quickly, and chances are good that you won't have time to see his super ego-sensitive side. He'll just disappear when he's angry or go off somewhere, trying to solve a problem. Also, Virgo is apt to keep his self-perceived faults under wraps.

Getting Through the Barrier

In fact, Virgo is only likely to fall in love with a person who can see past all his barriers and self-imposed walls. Though his dream is to be uncovered, he'll never admit it. He's even less likely to let you in if he doesn't want to. In fact, he can be downright antisocial. You may find it frustrating when he calls it a night just when you're supposed to meet up with your friends.

Essential

Part of the reason Virgo is likely to fall into a depression has to do with the way he keeps his emotions bottled up. When he finally releases them, it's like a torrential storm: unexpected and powerful.

Then again, if Virgo trusts you—really trusts you—you've won a true, reliable friend and lover. Though Virgo gives everyone a chance, it's not easy to win his real respect and loyalty.

And there's no one who will be there for you like Virgo. He does everything necessary to get the job done. He's efficient, he's reliable, and he knows just the right thing to say to cheer you up. In fact, you'd think Virgo is a rock. Don't be fooled—he's strong, but he also suffers in silence.

A Battle Within

Virgo wavers between paranoia and excessive trust. Fortunately, she's bright, funny, witty, and refined. Like Scorpio and Leo, though, Virgo believes people are either with her or against her. But unlike Scorpio and Leo, who go more by a sense of skin, Virgo tries to rationalize things away. She can't help dissecting things. A less mature Virgo will analyze every move of her love partner, right down to the way he says, "Let's talk later."

Here's the rub: Virgo doesn't want you to know that she's a real softie. She loves love and wants to be smitten ten times over. But she can't shake the feeling that she needs to protect herself.

🅔 Alert

Out of all the signs in the zodiac, don't get on the bad side of Virgo. Like Scorpio, Capricorn, or Gemini, she can get nasty or vengeful. Virgo won't completely forgive, and she certainly won't forget.

Scared of Love?

Virgo is cursed with a fear of love. Many times, she even pushes prospective love mates away unwittingly because she's afraid of what a real love match might mean. She'd have to be open. Exposed. Vulnerable. This is Virgo's biggest hurdle.

A younger, less evolved Virgo, unfortunately, is also likely to get involved with an emotional or physically abusive partner. Though almost all Virgos seem mature at a very young age, it usually takes a while for a Virgo to truly grow emotionally. For this reason, many Virgos find their real love mates in their thirties, or even later (in some cases), instead of in their twenties.

The Art of Attraction

Here's an important thing to remember. The only way to get a Virgo to truly fall in love with you is to make sure he knows he can depend on you. He needs to trust you. And he's likely to "save you"—it's in his blood. Plus, you cannot be a pushover. Virgo needs excitement on the scale of wildfire. You have to stimulate his senses as well as his brain. Virgo loves to laugh. He has a great sense of humor, but few can make him really laugh out loud. If you can, you've got an ace in the hole. Also remember that Virgo is an Earth sign and, not surprisingly, needs to work hard. Financial security is a necessity to him, and he can overdo it at times.

Long Haul

Virgo women have an instinctive nurturing side. They make great mothers because they know when to be affectionate and when to discipline. Though she tends to be a pushover with her kids—she spoils them—a Virgo woman is not likely to be overshadowed or undermined by her mate. A good husband for Virgo is one who knows to leave the details of raising their progeny to her. She knows just the right way to do it, and he trusts her good sense. Instead, Virgo wants her partner to be there more for her. She needs the support only he can give her in order for her to run the family the way it should be.

 **Essential**

> Those thinking of taking Virgo as a mate should be aware that Virgo has a possessive side when it comes to family. He wants control of the children, as well as full attention of his wife. In other words, everyone must look to him for guidance.

The Little Stuff Counts

Virgo men and women both tend to be attracted to a subtle sexiness. They like refinement in a mate and can't stand showoffs. Instead, Virgo believes, sexiness should come from within. A Virgo woman will notice the way her man dresses—and she'll expect him to suit up accordingly, depending on what they have planned. In other words, she'll want him to dress well if they're supposed to meet the parents that day, but she'll be just as happy to see him in an old button-down and jeans for a long car trip. Just keep in mind that the Virgo woman will notice what you choose to wear for which occasion.

The Virgo man isn't quite as picky about how his woman dresses. He'll be more interested, instead, in seeing whether she listens to and respects what he says. All Virgos will be highly offended if a mate asks the same question two or three times. For a Virgo, words are very important. He'll listen closely to what you say, and he'll expect you to do the same for him.

Pillow Talk: Signs in the Bedroom

Virgo needs a strong mate who can stand up to her. Most Virgos are verbally powerful, and they expect the same of their partners. The Virgo woman is likely to be attracted to men who can help lighten up her outlook on life and herself. She's usually drawn to those who can lessen her load of responsibilities. Her life is tough enough; she wants her relationship to be problem-free. She despises arguing, but some people just rub her the wrong way. Also, both the Virgo man and Virgo woman only go to bed with someone who they feel respects and cares for them—more than just physically.

The Secret Virgo Man

Here's a tip: Both Virgo men and women hate being a slave to their own passions, but they love sex. They just try not to admit it sometimes. For the Virgo man (as for the Virgo woman), sex is a process. He sometimes doesn't see a good thing even when it's standing in front of him. He's not a big romantic in the early stages. Things need to build for him. For a woman to grab his heart, she can't be too available to him, but she can't let him ignore her either—he'll pull away at a moment's notice. He'll test her, too, and see how much he can get away with.

Encouragement

Unlike a Virgo woman, a Virgo man is a bit unsure of his bedroom prowess. His woman should use words to restore his confidence. Then she should pull away a bit and let him work for her. With the Virgo man, it's always push-pull. To seduce him into bed, a few well-placed words will tell him that you're interested.

The Secret Virgo Woman

On the other hand, a Virgo woman will be very influenced with hints here and there before the actual act. Make her think about what languorous, beautiful sex could be like and let that stew in her brain for a while. Unfortunately, you won't necessarily know whether a Virgo woman is interested in you. She usually plays it cool and doesn't like to wear her heart on her sleeve.

Similarly, if she cries or has an emotional outburst, it doesn't necessarily mean it concerns you. Get to the bottom of the situation and you'll thank yourself later.

Sensual and Sexual

A Virgo woman is sensual and sexual. She loves having her hair stroked and her feet rubbed. She loves massages, too. Though she's as naughty as the rest of us, she likes creating a "good girl" image for those around her, sometimes. Ask a Virgo woman for anything showy or extra kinky and—guaranteed— you will absolutely never see her again. Though she sometimes falls for the rogue, she really wants to be seduced with sweetness at the heart of it all.

Sun Love Matches

Virgo can be a contradiction in terms. Though he longs for security, he sometimes goes for the truly unattainable. Why? A less mature Virgo subconsciously seeks to punish himself and learn from the experience. He longs to understand the world and the way it works—shooting for the stars (or, on the negative side, choosing a mate who's completely wrong for him): It seems to be all part of a bigger plan to him. Strangely, he's attracted to many different kinds of partners. But Virgo tends to stay in bad relationships longer than he should because he's determined to make it work. Fortunately, a more mature Virgo is quite rational. When he finally finds the right partner—"The One"—he could choose wisely. As an Earth sign, Virgo pairs well with other Earth signs. He sometimes gets along well with Air and with other analytical signs, depending on how much they're willing to give as much as they take from Virgo.

Read on to discover the love combinations for the Virgo woman.

Virgo Man

When two Virgos get together, gone are the terms "compromise" and "middle ground." They either get along famously, or they're at each other's throats. True, a little bickering can sometimes be good foreplay. For them, though, when neither is willing to back down, a simple "harmless" argument can escalate into a full-blown fight. At the other end of the spectrum, the Virgo man and woman instinctively understand each other. They usually know how to make each other happy. Once they start recounting their day or telling stories to each other, fun and laughter consume them. In bed, they let down their guards completely and can have "soul" sex—powerful, intense, and even a bit wild. All in all, this can be a good long-term relationship, with a possible marriage ahead, but only if the two can remain in synch.

Essential

Virgo has a tendency to be antisocial. This actually works for her in a relationship. Together, the Virgo man and woman can stay home or just spend quiet nights out somewhere at a little neighborhood place. Fortunately, their living styles are very similar.

Libra Man

Libra can be a heartbreaker for the Virgo woman. He's dangerous for her. She tries not to let him fascinate her, but she just can't seem to help herself. He's got that sexiness within. She thinks she can win him over and make him faithful only to her. Maybe she can, but it's not easy. The Libra man knows he can rile up the Virgo woman. Sometimes he does it for fun, and other times he does it because he's not sure what he wants. This drives Virgo crazy. Though she should blame him for inconsistency, she usually blames herself. In bed, though, these two go together extremely well. If Libra dedicates himself to Virgo and doesn't mind "lightening up" Virgo, this can be a possible long-term relationship, with marriage a possibility . . . if the Virgo woman can keep her cool. However, it may make her go off the deep end first.

Scorpio Man

The Virgo woman barely skims the surface in trying to get to know the Scorpio man. She looks in the wrong places. In fact, she doesn't quite know how to deal with him. Virgo may just lose her mind trying to analyze Scorpio's moods. She can't keep up with him. She's also more practical. Fortunately, both like to analyze, and gradually they find that they get along wonderfully. Their differences keep them bound and fascinated. These two can be good in bed together if Virgo lets down her emotional guard. Then he'll really make her knees weak. This can be a possible long-term relationship and maybe even a good marriage. It's been done many times—but the Virgo woman craves security and the Scorpio man changes his feelings frequently.

Sagittarius Man

The Virgo woman intrigues the Sagittarius man. She seems to know what she wants, and he likes that. They may even go away on a little weekend trek together. If so, that's when the problems start. Though Virgo is sexually attracted to the male Archer and she likes his style, she questions him a bit too much. And even though Virgo mostly just likes to play devil's advocate, Sagittarius can get easily offended when she doesn't take his words to heart.

She also reduces him to little arguments (however small), and this bothers him. In bed, Virgo's in for a wild ride. He goes more by instinct, though, and she would prefer to hear how he feels from his own mouth. Sag usually speaks through silence and movements. This is a possible long-term relationship, though not a likely marriage, unless the stars (unusually) align for them.

❓ Question

What's the biggest downfall with a relationship between Virgo and Sagittarius?
Too many personal questions will make Sagittarius flee. Virgo wants to know about his past—she's curious. Sagittarius hates answering things about himself. Her curiosity is too much, too aggressive, too fast.

Capricorn Man

Finally, the Virgo woman has found a man who can ground her. Capricorn helps Virgo with her responsibilities and can come off like a father figure at times. Though Virgo can't stand the father act, she does respect Capricorn and believes what he says. Virgo instinctively trusts Capricorn, which she should. The Capricorn man, though, is a little wary of the Virgo woman. He senses her emotional capacity underneath it all, and it scares him. Also, he knows he'll have a tough time controlling her. In bed, these two make a sizzling match. If the Virgo woman can let the Goat tell her what to do—and if she manages to listen—they can make a very good long-term partnership. Virgo likes to banter and discuss; Cap can sometimes get defensive when she does. They have an okay chance for marriage as long as Virgo takes "the word of the Goat" seriously.

Aquarius Man

These two get along really well. Virgo and Aquarius make each other laugh, and Aquarius has enough of a laid-back attitude to make Virgo feel at ease. Though Virgo doesn't know whether she should rely on the Aquarius man, she believes she can. This may or may not be true. Aquarius is definitely one of a kind. But Aquarius doesn't have any hidden agendas. In fact, Aquarius will get annoyed if Virgo doubts his true intentions (even if they're not good ones). In bed, Aquarius is the first to really open up Virgo. They can get pretty creative between the sheets. If Virgo doesn't get too serious with Aquarius right away, this can be a probable long-term relationship. It's also a very possible marriage, especially if Aquarius doesn't rely too heavily on Virgo for work-related issues.

Pisces Man

The Pisces man has a quiet strength that the Virgo woman admires. She likes his odd and quirky sense of humor and knows he's intelligent. This time, though, it's the Pisces man who's not sure if he can trust the Virgo woman. He sees her spinning her wheels and wonders why she lets the little things bother her. He's famous for seeing the big picture. Though he tries desperately to help her come to the same conclusions, these two always seem to wind up on separate pages (though the fantasy of that can be quite alluring for a while).

ⓔ✷ Essential

> The Pisces man always has a kind of otherworldly sense about him. He's born with wisdom about psychology and the way things work (not all Pisces men, but most) beyond his years. Though Virgo appreciates this, she doesn't quite understand why. She winds up telling him what to do. Instead, she should listen to him more carefully.

Also, they move at two different rates in the relationship. Virgo may be ready to commit before he is. He goes by instinct; she's planning. When they make it to bed, though, their mating will be slow and sensual. However, Virgo may want more of a warrior type sexually than sensual Pisces is. This match may be a decent bet for the long term, though it's not really a recommended marriage, unless these two want it badly enough (they do find each other fascinating).

Aries Man

The Virgo woman amuses the Aries man—in a good way. He backs her up in her little tiffs with this person and that. Though he picks his fights more carefully, he admires her nevertheless for standing up for herself. In the beginning, the Aries man makes Virgo think she's found the love of a lifetime. He's romantic and passionate, and she can actually feel herself falling—but too late. By the time she's hooked for real, he may be on to his next conquest. It depends how mature he is and if he's able to give Virgo time to open up and let him really know her. If Virgo can go in with the right frame of mind, and Aries is serious about giving her a chance, this can be a possible long-term relationship. It's also a possible marriage—it's been done—though it may be a dangerous one in terms of Virgo getting what she needs: security for a lifetime (unless Aries is willing to give it).

Taurus Man

Many times the Virgo woman is the Taurus man's ideal—at least so he thinks. Though she's not as old-fashioned as she seems, she passes as the kind of gal the Taurus man wants to marry. The only problem is that the Taurus man hates confrontation of any kind. When the Virgo woman wants a straight answer, he runs away—or scoots around it. If she lets the issue go, he'll come back to her with a response in due time. If she persists, he'll label her as a troublemaker and go off in search of greener, more tranquil pastures. However, if the two can be sensitive with each other's feelings, this can be a probable long-term relationship. They also have a good chance for marriage, though there may not be enough levity and playfulness to carry the relationship forever.

🅔❗ Alert

When they go out, Virgo loves the fact that Taurus is generous. And if there's anyone who can get Virgo going in bed, it's the Bull. Sexually, they can work.

Gemini Man

These two can get into tons of mischief together—they actually egg each other on. They make each other laugh. The Gemini man likes to rely on the Virgo woman. Unfortunately, the Virgo woman can be more sensitive than the Gemini man. This can get in the way of their communication. In fact, the two sometimes misunderstand each other terribly. Gemini makes Virgo paranoid, and Virgo weighs Gemini down. Gemini also needs to do what he says he's going to. If he doesn't, Virgo is going to wonder if Gemini is even more flighty than he seems to be. Virgo doesn't necessarily trust him. In bed, they can have fun if Gemini can prove it's not just a fling or if Virgo concedes that it is just that. This can be a possible long-term relationship and even marriage. It's been done and can work if Gemini has his feet on the ground.

Cancer Man

The Cancer man brings out Virgo's emotional side. Though he can appear to be superficial, which Virgo usually is not, she forgives him and gets to know his deeper side over time. The Virgo woman, however, is stronger than the Cancer man—or she appears to be. If she can let down her strong (sometimes harsh) exterior, these two could get along. But since Cancer operates on a different spiritual level than Virgo, they may never fully click into place. In bed, the two can experiment and find new sexual adventures. But that's only if Virgo can be more subtle in her approach. Also, Cancer shies away from conflict. They may find a very precarious middle ground, though, so this can be a possible long-term relationship but not a very probable marriage . . . unless Cancer's Mom was just like her: a strange possibility.

Leo Man

A Leo woman and a Virgo man? Perhaps it can work. How about a Virgo woman with a Leo man? Well . . . she knows how to give a good, honest compliment, and the Leo man knows he can rely on her when he needs her. He admires her for her wit and smarts. However, he can't make up his mind if she's the love of his life or someone who will lead to his downfall. As friends, they're unconquerable. Sexually, they may go well together as long as Virgo lets Leo lead. This is a possible long-term relationship, and can also perhaps be a good marriage. However, the Virgo woman must find a way to not continually burst Leo's secret idealistic bubble and must let him have his way some of the time.

Love Planets: Venus and Mercury

A little Virgo in your chart will make it easier for you to understand the motives of other people. It may make you a bit abrasive.

You could stand to soften your ideals and outlook somewhat—but it will also give you insight into the human condition. A certain critical nature enters the picture here, too—one that you turn on yourself and on others. With Virgo in any star or planet, you should be aware of being too hard on yourself. If you're not kind and forgiving with yourself, who else is going to be? Here, discover the intricacies of Virgo in your chart.

ⓔ✳ Essential

Venus in Virgo has a tendency to let moods affect her. When she's happy, she jokes, laughs, and is easy to get along with. When she's not, she can pick fights or argue just for the sake of it.

Venus in Virgo

Love is important to you even though you spend more time alone than you'd like. With you, love is all or nothing. Security is also important to you. True, you stay in a doomed relationship longer than you should, but you don't have any delusions. You know whether it's going to work. The actual location you have sex is actually very important to you. First, you like to decide where it is you're going to consummate—your place, his, or elsewhere. Venus in Virgo is paired well with Venus in Virgo, Taurus, Aquarius, Libra, and Scorpio.

Mercury in Virgo

You're self-critical and wish you weren't. You also tend to be paranoid about what others think of you. Mercury in Virgo, though, helps you analyze those around you. It's a wonderful sign for those who write, study, or are interested in music. You remember conversations and lyrics to songs you heard only once. This could also affect you in love—you long to hear just the right thing at just the right moment. You can't help yourself when a heated debate is going on—you either walk away or get right in the middle. Your partner needs to be intelligent and must have good rationalization skills or you easily get bored. On the other hand, you like a mate with a touch of "simple." Also, someone who can lighten your moods and your affinity for self-pity is a welcome friend or partner. Mercury in Virgo goes well with Mercury in Aries, Aquarius, Taurus, and Libra.

CHAPTER 7

Libra

Libra in love is a wonderful thing to behold—his eyes twinkle; he has a spring in his step. He has an innate sexiness and purity that comes through with each smile he throws your way. But he's a lot more complicated than he seems. In this chapter, discover the real Libra and what he may be hiding behind his good looks.

How Can You Win Over Charming Libra?

1. **Growing up, Libra man was probably:**
   A. Sitting alone in the library
   B. Always telling jokes to friends
   C. Hanging out with the teachers
   D. Cutting class and getting into trouble

2. **How do Libras feel about an aggressive mate?**
   A. They love it.
   B. They don't like it.
   C. They like it sometimes.
   D. They don't have a preference.

3. **Is it possible for Libras to separate sex from love?**
   A. Never, even if they want to
   B. Definitely, if they want to
   C. They try to but can't
   D. They think they can . . . but then actually fall in love

4. **What will Libra most likely do in a heated debate?**
   A. Get right into the thick of it
   B. Wait for an in . . . then go for it!
   C. Yell until everyone quiets down
   D. Bow out graciously

5. **If you had to pick one negative trait, you can count on Libra sometimes to be:**
   A. Snobby
   B. Unfair
   C. Indecisive
   D. Rude

6. **A 24-year-old Libra guy is standing in front of four potential would-be girlfriends. Which one would he pick (without knowing them)?**
    A. The beautiful older woman, a seductress
    B. The pretty, young virgin
    C. The sexy vamp type around his age
    D. The gorgeous European exchange student

7. **Does Libra like to be in charge?**
    A. Definitely
    B. Definitely not

8. **What do Libra men think about their wardrobes?**
    A. They're guys. They don't care!
    B. Each piece is hand-picked to perfection.
    C. They make it look "free and easy" but care a great deal.
    D. They care a little . . . but if things don't look good, that's okay, too.

9. **Libra is ruled by the planet:**
    A. Saturn
    B. Mercury
    C. Venus
    D. Jupiter

10. **Liev Schreiber, Michael Douglas, and Tim Robbins . . . What do these three Libra men have in common?**
    A. They have all had long relationships with Libra women at one point.
    B. They have all cheated on their wives.
    C. They all prefer the bachelor life.
    D. They have all had drinking problems at one point.

Answers: 1. b, 2. b, 3. b, 4. d, 5. c, 6. b, 7. a, 8. c, 9. c, 10. a

Libra, the Fair

There are two ways to explain this title. First, he is fair in a physical sense—nice to look at. Second, he's fair: He needs to weigh out and decipher all the implications of things. Let's deal with the first.

The Libra man is almost always handsome on some level. The Libra woman has her own beauty. You would think Libra would be cocky about his good fortune in the looks department, but he's not. He also has a sweetness that makes him seem vulnerable. But that's not as simple as it seems, either. Instead, he looks to gain stability and security through other things—some of those worthwhile and some not.

❓ Question

Is Libra a fair judge of character?
It's hard to say. A more evolved Libra will weigh out the benefits and disadvantages of a friendship/love relationship and will come to a pretty solid conclusion. A less evolved Libra will let fear get in the way of his good sense.

In other words, Libra's position in life—who he is, where he comes from, who his friends are, and whom he's seen with—are important to Libra deep down. Though he doesn't come off as an opportunist, there's something very odd about Libra's social life. He has friends in different corners of the world but is extremely selective about the people he'll get close to. You'll probably notice that Libra takes everything and everyone with a grain of salt. He has many friends but doesn't necessarily consider them real ones. It's a mistake for most people to think they know the real Libra. He's pensive and is constantly assessing situations in his head. But, for the most part, Libra pretty much tells it straight.

Mature Versus Immature Libra

There are two very different kinds of Libras: mature and deeply immature. Age is not a factor. As a rule of thumb, although there are always exceptions, Libra women tend to come into their own far earlier than Libra men. A mature Libra will approach you directly, have a conversation with you, and get to the heart of the matter. You'll feel like he's listened to and heard what you said. A less mature Libra will strike you as confident, interesting, and somewhat mysterious. He'll go around a topic and let you do more of the talking—seemingly hoping that you'll somehow say the wrong thing. Or he'll simply provoke you, saying things he knows will either infuriate you or make you turn away from him.

Libra has emotional depth, but he doesn't know how to manage his feelings. He's also insecure, though he doesn't show it one bit. It's best to stay away from him until he understands what's important and what's not.

Eye of the Storm

Libra needs to be in control of her own destiny. If she feels pressured or sucked into something she doesn't want to be a part of, she instantly backs away. She also needs to decide when she wants to get romantically caught up and when she doesn't. For Libra, timing is everything.

She's also idealistic in a way that's not particularly romantic. Though she can be incredibly romantic and sweet—deep down, Libra is a real poet—she saves this for the person of her dreams. And just who is that? If a less mature Libra were to decide, she would create or invent a mate for herself. He'd be handsome and sexy, sweet, kind, smart, witty, bashful, modest, deep . . . the list goes on.

Libra also tends (unwittingly) to create problems around her, but then scoots away before everything gets too heated. In this way, she's like the eye of the storm—seemingly calm right in the middle of it all while bedlam, chaos, and tornado drama happens around her.

Essential

Libra is pretty sure what kind of partner she wants. Though she's known to be fair, that's not always true when it comes to picking a mate. Libra is determined to find someone who fits the perfect image she has in her head.

The Art of Attraction

Libra may be difficult to conquer. The Libra man, for example, usually goes for the prettiest girl in the room. But tastes vary: What's beautiful to one may not appeal to another. At the very least, Libras tend to be born with a good aesthetic sense. A Libra who incorporates his love of beauty into his everyday life is more balanced than a Libra who seeks perfection from the people around him.

Aside from that, Libra doesn't like his potential mate to be too aggressive. Courting, to a Libra, is like a dance—a tango, perhaps—slow and intricate. Libra is also a subtle flirt, but he doesn't like his partner to be too flirty with others. Though he's not as jealous as some other signs (like Leo or Cancer), he still doesn't like to compete with others for your attention.

Though Libra does like to be swept away with love, he can also get involved on a more superficial level. Libra, remember, is an Air sign . . . he can rationalize anything away. If a Libra decides he wants to have a fling, he has it—with no regrets. How do you know if Libra is playing with you or playing for keeps? Easy. Just ask him. Libra will tell you. He's not known to hide his intentions. In fact, he's as straight as they come.

❓ Question

What's the biggest problem in conquering a Libra? Indecision. Libra doesn't get involved until he's 100 percent sure about you. And sometimes it takes him a while to decide if he wants to risk it or not.

The Long Haul

Libra gets married either very late or very early. There's almost never a middle ground. Those who settle down early in life tend to choose poorly and may later regret it. Normally, though, when Libra finally marries, it's for keeps. He devotes himself to his other half and relies on her for sustenance. He can also be affectionate in private. Most Libras aren't keen to public displays of affection. They like to keep their home life at home.

Because Libra can easily separate romantic or sexual flings from real love and someone he intends to stay with, you should expect him to act accordingly. If it's a temporary love situation, he won't hesitate to cheat or look around while he's with you. If he wants you for keeps, though, he'll be faithful and true.

The Little Stuff Counts

While Virgo is more detail-oriented in noticing flaws in others, Libra, too, will pay attention to the little things. Libra men, for example, always go for women who are particularly well groomed. This doesn't mean that she has to be elegant or even always dressed up. The Libra man likes women who can be casual with a pair of jeans, too.

Though Libra likes out-there sexiness in a partner for a fling, he tends to lean to the more conservative side in hunting for a future mate. The Libra woman also likes a man who seems capable and rock steady. Libra is very good at accomplishing whatever task he puts his mind to—whether it's rock climbing, flying a plane, or selling ice to an Eskimo. Unlike Gemini, he doesn't talk to fill in the gaps. He likes a partner to understand the benefits of silence.

Pillow Talk: Signs in the Bedroom

How much a Libra suffers earlier on in life will normally determine how mature she is. Libras who grow up with a sense of discipline and are not spoiled will be quite evolved. This carries over to the bedroom. A less mature Libra man, for example, will need to feel completely in charge in bed. He'll pick a woman who is demure or inexperienced for a long-term mate. For a fling, he'll choose a woman whose tastes run on the kinky side.

All Libras love sex. Actually, their libidos may even be the biggest in the zodiac. They also have a hidden side (like Virgo does) that only comes out with either partners they feel comfortable with or partners they don't think they'll keep around for long. Verbally, they like to test out a partner.

The Secret Libra Man

Many times, the Libra man will speak with his eyes. Though he talks a good game and he might even be touchy-feely, this means nothing. You'll know if a Libra man is serious about you by the way he looks at you—it'll be different from the way he looks at others. His eyes have the power to pierce your soul. You'll feel it in your gut.

Essential

If you're seducing a Libra man, let him seduce you. If you've already been intimate with him, you can be bolder. Stare into his eyes and touch his chest softly. He'll melt.

One good way to capture a Libra man is to let him come to you. Ignore him a little, but always be polite. He'll be waiting for you on your doorstep when you come home. Also remember that Libra is expecting you to make the wrong move. He'll watch you from afar and even have his friends keep an eye on you. Libras are notorious observers when it comes to love. Any indecent or inappropriate behavior—including excessive flirting or affection with the opposite sex—will turn a Libra off pronto.

The Secret Libra Woman

She likes men who are skilled in the art of making love. To her, sex is really art, and it must be beautiful in some way. This doesn't mean that she must always be in love to make love. On the contrary, the Libra woman is just as good at separating the real thing from a sexual adventure. Though she prefers to be completely swept away in love, she's capable of having fun, too.

The Libra woman tends to be quite independent. She can sometimes be more aggressive in bed than the Libra man. She knows what she wants and usually gets it. Though she can be a heartbreaker, she always tells it straight. She won't lead you on, for example, if she doesn't intend to follow through. Though it might take her a little while to decide, once she does, she's crystal clear.

e✔ Fact

> The Libra woman tends to have lots of energy. This carries over into the bedroom as well. She'll look for a partner who wants to go all night—not one who seems to think that "foreplay" is an expression used in golf.

Sun Love Matches

Libra tends to be slippery in love. He's hard to catch and even harder to figure out. Because Libra can be idealistic about what kind of partner he wants, it's difficult to get into his head and know just what he's looking for. Do keep in mind that Libra always has a set image of what he wants. He's not going to change his ideas on a whim.

Read on to learn about compatible matches for the Libra woman.

Libra Man

This is a hard match to predict—but with incredible potential. If there's a lot of Earth in the rest of their charts (one or both), they go together fabulously. The Libra woman, though, may take the lead, and this may irk the Libra man (who likes to feel like he's in control of things—even if he's not). The couple actually works better when the Libra woman steers the boat. This also has to do with a question of timing. If both are ready for something serious, they can be a majestic couple together.

In bed, things are creative and adventurous. They really "get" each other. In fact, again, if the Libra man lets the Libra woman get her way, this partnership can be headed for greatness. Overall, this is a probable long-term relationship with an excellent chance for marriage.

Scorpio Man

The Scorpio man enchants the Libra woman at first. What bothers her, though, is that even if she usually gets a straight answer from him, she senses he's hiding something. The Scorpio man, too, doesn't seem as grounded as Libra would like. He plays games and can easily give her a guilt trip. Plus, he's moody. Though the sex can be fantastic, Libra is more creative while Scorpio is more intense. These two can really laugh together, though. This can be a possible long-term relationship, with marriage possible on the horizon. However, Scorpio's dark moods must be kept at bay for that to happen . . . otherwise, Libra will jump ship. (Scorpio may just push her overboard first.)

Sagittarius Man

The male Archer doesn't like to show how much he needs the company of a loving woman. He gets a bit stressed when things don't go his way, and the Libra woman doesn't quite understand how to handle him. She may need a softer touch and less talking to fill in the blanks. Sagittarius also needs her to boost his ego in bed. He's a lusty lover—she is, too—but he goes more by instinct. Intellectually, they inspire each other. But if Sag doesn't trust her fully, he'll run faster than you can say the word "bye." This can be a possible long-term relationship and a possible marriage, but not necessarily of the soul mate variation.

Capricorn Man

Capricorn and Libra can get into power struggles. She needs to let him lead. Also, the Capricorn man may not be refined enough for the Libra lady. If he is out to please her—going where she wants and dressing as she likes—they'll get along fine. Tough, that! Though Capricorn likes to dress (and be) more informal than Libra, they don't have too many problems finding a middle ground. In bed, Capricorn absolutely needs to dominate, and the Libra woman is usually more than willing, in this case, to let him do so. This can be a very possible long-term relationship, with marriage possible, too. If Cap remains open—not so "black and white" and stubborn about the way things are—Libra will cherish the security he can provide.

Aquarius Man

An Aquarius man and a Libra woman? Who would've thought? The two are different in so many ways even though they're both Air signs. (Yes, Aquarius is an Air sign, not a water sign.) Somehow, though, they can balance each other out—sometimes. Though Libra is more conservative than Aquarius, he inspires her to be more creative. In return, she teaches him about art and the finer things in life. In bed, they have similar styles, and it sizzles. Aquarius may be a bit kinkier, though. This can be a very possible long-term relationship. It's also a possible marriage. However, it really depends on the couple: Libra is a sensitive soul, while Aquarius tends to be out-there gregarious and possibly not as couple-oriented, sometimes, as Libra may like.

Alert

The Aquarius man has an unfaithful streak. If he's committed to being faithful with a Libra woman, this can work. If not, Libra will walk!

Pisces Man

To Libra, the Pisces man is just plain weird—but she likes that. Though she gets the feeling that he's just going along with everything she says, she doesn't mind it at all. Art seems to be a common theme between these two. They're also both quite conservative in their manner. The success of this match depends on whether Pisces can stand up to Libra. If he's a dreamer, Libra will get frustrated. If he's as independent as she is, they'll get along well. However, bed is another matter. Pisces may not be able to keep up with Libra's energy. Also, if Pisces's mood swings become too much for her, Libra will become flustered and lose her cool. Both can be indecisive about getting to the altar. This can be a possible long-term partnership. Marriage isn't probable, but it's not impossible, either: It's been done before with success.

Aries Man

The Aries man swaggers in and charms the charming Libra woman. She fascinates him; he fascinates her. But the Aries man needs to be the center of attention, and the Libra woman gets the spotlight without even trying. Aries holds her back, somehow. He also miffs her with all his bluster and loud antics in restaurants. (She hates public scenes.) She'll get annoyed when he doesn't stick to his word—which she does—or if he shows up late again with excuses. At least he's got all the right words. They can have a great affair if the Aries man respects the Libra woman—completely. All in all, this can be a great fling, whether it's short-term or even a little longer. It's just not a probable marriage. Again, though, only two people in love can decide.

Taurus Man

Though Taurus is likely to fall in love first, the Libra woman will keep him reeled in until she feels it herself. These two inspire each other and are dynamic together. Libra has all kinds of moral and honorable behavior that Taurus admires. The only problem the two could have, however, is Taurus's thin skin: Libra criticizes and Taurus shrinks away in humiliation. Plus, he won't confront the situation. However, when he finally gives it back, it's her turn to try to calm the beast (him). Good luck with that! In bed, they make a perfect match. If Libra can impress Taurus with her strong hold on finances, this can be a probable long-term relationship with a good chance for marriage. She'll just have to recognize that he's not as mature as she thought he was—and appreciate him for what he is: potent and compelling, but a child (at times).

Gemini Man

Gemini and Libra together are the most wild, fun, and out-rageous couple in the room. Just don't get in between these two—their bond is strong and ferocious. Though Gemini is more possessive and jealous than the Libra woman, the gender combination here can work (Gemini man, Libra woman). The other way around may be a bit more difficult. Though Gemini can get kinkier in bed, Libra can keep up if she wants to. If they can each accept the little skeletons hidden in their respective closets, this can be a good long-term love and a probable marriage, too. However, the Libra woman must trust and respect him completely for that to happen.

🅴❗ Alert

Gemini should beware of asking too many questions of Libra! She doesn't like giving away too many personal things about her life right away. When Gemini interrogates too quickly, Libra gets wary of Gemini. She doesn't like the feeling that she's being judged.

Cancer Man

Cancer and Libra are seemingly from two different planets. Though they can have a wonderful friendship—talking for hours about the strange and unusual—it may end there. Cancer feels. Libra thinks. Cancer doesn't rationalize; Libra does nothing but. If the Libra woman can always swing Cancer's opinion to her side, this has a chance. Sexually, though, the Cancer man may not completely understand what the Libra woman needs—but she's still quite taken. If he's willing to let her shine and doesn't get too possessive, this could work. Most likely, though, this is a possible long-term relationship and not a probable marriage. The two together must decide.

Leo Man

Leo and Libra? They're both passionate—but about completely different things. Leo is passionate about love, whereas Libra gets more excited about life in general. He takes romance more seriously. She likes her independence. Leo is unduly impressed with the way Libra follows through with everything. Libra loves the fact that Leo is warm and generous, and treats her with respect. Both have a love of beauty in all things. If she has some Fire signs in the rest of her chart, this can be a possible long-term relationship. It's not a probable marriage, but it is possible. However, the planets would have to align just right for this match.

🅔✴ Essential

In bed their relationship can work only if Libra lets Leo have all the control. Out of bed, though, she needs to set some serious boundaries for the Leo man. This is the only way he will fall in love with her (and only her), truly.

Virgo Man

When these two get together, watch out! They can either click completely or rub each other the wrong way, causing chaos around them. Talk about verbal warfare—these two can fight dirty. And though this will inevitably turn the Virgo man on, the Libra woman will probably head for the hills. In bed, though, there is no more perfect lover for the Libra woman. They heat each other up and adore each other's style. If the Virgo man can soften a little and Libra can hold back the judgmental comments (ditto for Virgo), this can be a possible long-term situation. It's also a very possible marriage.

Love Planets: Venus and Mercury

Libra in your chart always gives someone a little mystique—charm, beauty from within, and a certain aura of ingenuity. It also makes you consider your options before diving in, positioning them against one another to understand whether the advantages outweigh the disadvantages. Also, Libra is always attracted to beauty in some way: through art, people, or surroundings.

Venus in Libra

More than anything, a person with Venus in Libra loves being in love. Though you're highly selective about a mate—picky even—you don't like being alone for long stretches of time. No one can force you to do what you don't want, and the worst thing a partner could do is pressure you to make a decision you're not ready to make. Venus in Libra goes well with Venus in Libra, Taurus, Virgo, and Capricorn.

Fact

> You're very versatile in bed and in life. You seek the perfect balance from a love mate: interesting, kind, gentle, sweet, and smart. You look for a best friend and lover, someone who you've probably envisioned even before meeting them.

Mercury in Libra

Intellectually, you're a smart cookie, and you're resourceful, too. Your know-how doesn't just come from books—it comes from doing. Besides being familiar with literature, you've got what they call "street smarts." People like to hear you talk because you know what makes a good story, and you're not keen on exaggerating. Talking about love may be your only downfall. You sometimes give too much away when you talk about a partner. This could be embarrassing to others or make you seem a bit flighty. No matter, though. You're still charming and fabulous—and deep down you know it (without ever giving off a pretentious or even a slightly cocky air). Mercury in Libra goes well with Mercury in Gemini, Virgo, Libra, and Sagittarius.

CHAPTER 8

Scorpio

Scorpio has sex appeal off the charts. When he falls in love, it's deeply and utterly. The only problem is getting him there—and then keeping him. In this chapter, find out how to figure out dark and mysterious Scorpio.

How Do You Capture Scorpio's Protected Heart?

1. **What is the Scorpio man's style of dating after he's pretty sure about a woman?**
   A. He continues on with the same pace.
   B. He prefers a woman to chase him a bit now.
   C. He only likes the chase—and ends it.
   D. He goes overboard, sending gifts, etc.

2. **Scorpios fear something in love. What is it?**
   A. Getting emotional
   B. Being discovered
   C. Meeting the in-laws
   D. Living with a partner

3. **Scorpios are known for:**
   A. Having a good memory
   B. Being jealous
   C. Getting revenge
   D. All of the above

4. **Scorpios ask "what?" all the time when you say something. Why?**
   A. They don't understand what you said.
   B. They don't really care what you said.
   C. They're notorious for bad hearing.
   D. They hear what they want to hear.

5. **Scorpio is a(n) ___ sign.**
   A. Water
   B. Fire
   C. Earth
   D. Air

6. **If Scorpio is dating you—but not in love—how will you know?**

    A. You won't: He'll act the same either way.

    B. He'll lie a lot.

    C. He'll run hot and cold.

    D. He'll tell you he's in love even when he's not.

7. **How do you get a Scorpio man to tell you the truth about another woman?**

    A. You give a scenario about another couple. He'll cave.

    B. You ask Scorpio; he'll tell you.

    C. You go to bed with him.

    D. He'll never tell.

8. **Which is not true for Scorpios?**

    A. Scorpios like neatness, but can sometimes be pack rats.

    B. Scorpios are private people, but hate being lonely.

    C. Scorpios will want to hear your secrets, but won't necessarily tell you theirs.

    D. Scorpios will keep pursuing a love interest, even when they're not that interested anymore.

9. **What may be considered a basic negative trait of Scorpio?**

    A. They're passive-aggressive.

    B. They're competitive.

    C. They're flaky.

    D. They're naive.

10. **Scorpio's sex drive may, at times, be tied to the ups and down of:**

    A. Love for you

    B. Passion for hobbies

    C. Work problems

    D. There's never a real reason

Answers: 1. b, 2. b, 3. d, 4. d, 5. a, 6. c, 7. b, 8. d, 9. a, 10. c

The Dark One

Scorpio always seems to have something dangerous about him. Perhaps you can't put your finger on it, but it's always there. He broods and mumbles under his breath, and you feel like he's always thinking. He also comes off as easygoing and free, though you know he's a force to deal with when he's angry—a virtual tornado when he actually lets loose.

Secretive

Yes, Scorpio always has something simmering just beneath the surface. He's crafty, and he knows how to make things go his way. Scorpio also speaks only half of what's on his mind. Most call him secretive, and he is. But there's something else—he's a private person. He's reserved. Though he comes off as friendly and open, Scorpio is very closed about the inner workings of his mind . . . more than he'll ever let on.

❷ Question

What do most Scorpios fear most?
Discovery. They're a little embarrassed about the oddities that go through their heads. Therefore, they're good at showing you only what they want you to see.

Proud

Scorpio is also a very proud creature. He's willful, stubborn, and determined to get his way. And the reason he's so hard to figure out is that he's more a contradiction in terms than most other signs of the zodiac. Here are a few examples:

- Scorpio tends to get more obsessed with someone who's not good for him (like Virgo).

- Scorpio will hunt down a potential mate, not relenting until she falls in love with him.
- Scorpio is a very private soul, but hates feeling lonely.
- Scorpio wants you to tell all your secrets, but won't tell any of his own. All Scorpios have something hidden in their past—they're not the open books they seem to be.
- Scorpio seems easygoing and cool one minute and then suddenly snaps, becoming anxious or angry.
- Scorpio overworks himself to the point of complete exhaustion, complains about it, but does nothing to resolve the problem.

Unpredictable

In short, Scorpio is, at the very least, entirely unpredictable. He's a mystery—that's for sure. So how do you snag Scorpio's heart? It's not easy. There are, however, some tricks and tips in this chapter. First, read up on what Scorpio is really thinking. Then, go to the section on love matches. By the end of these pages, you'll be a pro.

You're Mine

Okay, Scorpio is incredibly jealous and possessive, but she's also protective. A Scorpio will defend you within two inches of her life (the way Leo would). She's smart, and when she's in love—or believes she is—she's really in love. Fortunately, you can tell whether Scorpio is or isn't. In the beginning, he'll pursue you. He'll be generous and affectionate. When this behavior stops or wanes, you'll know you're starting to lose him.

Just keep in mind that a Scorpio will stay in a situation longer than he should. Because of this, when he breaks up, he usually does it in a harsh or uncaring way. This is done, really, to protect himself.

Alert

Think scorpion. Think deadly. Don't ever cross a Scorpio! She'll sneak up from behind. And she can be vengeful and crafty about it, knowing exactly how to push your buttons and possibly even hurt you.

Be advised, however, that when Scorpio finally ends it, it's over. You may be able to seduce her once or twice after, but only if she's convinced that you don't have any remaining feelings for her and are not looking for something more. This is the only way Scorpios show their practical side in love.

The Art of Attraction

Scorpio is all about transformation. Just associating with one will change your life in some way. While Aquarius, for example, may go for the strange or unique partner, Scorpio is drawn to opposites. He wants someone who can really go wild and let loose in the bedroom and then be able to dine among the best of them. Sex is also very important to Scorpio. He has the ability to make it good for both of you (a Scorpio woman, too).

In fact, the best time to have an important conversation is after lovemaking. He lets his guard down, and he'll be more willing to hear what you have to say. Get him to laugh a little before you start. Scorpio loves to laugh and does it too rarely. Incidentally, Scorpio is very orderly and clean, and he expects the same of you. Don't think of looking in his closet, though. Scorpio, though neat, is a notorious pack rat.

Fact

> Here's a tip: Scorpio men love to be complimented on inti-
> mate things like their clothes or their smell. So do Scorpio
> women. Give them a slow, sultry kiss and whisper a compli-
> ment in their ear. They'll love it.

The Long Haul

Scorpio can be difficult to deal with sometimes. He has certain unique requirements. Most likely, he likes to hang around
people his partner won't necessarily like or approve of. For this
reason, Scorpio tends to marry later than most. But Scorpio loves
love, and he wants to be in love forever. He loves children and can
make a wonderful, caring father who will do anything for his children (if he decides to have any). A Scorpio woman, too, has great
instincts with children. The only thing Scorpio must watch out for
is temper—most Scorpios have one. They let the anger build up
instead of releasing it, and it all comes out in a whoosh. Though
Scorpio would never in a million years willfully hurt a child, he
must be equally careful to keep this natural tendency at bay.

Is Scorpio in love with you? Not sure how he feels about
you? There is a subtle test you can give your Scorpio mate. It
does count as game playing, but if you really need to know, just
flirt with one of his friends. At the very least, he'll tell you about
all his friend's bad points (hoping to assure himself at the winner's place, next to you). At the very worst, he'll haul you out of
the restaurant and kiss you senseless so that you know for sure
whom you really belong to. Scorpio is one of the most jealous
signs. It's a sneaky way to snatch him and, perhaps, a manipulative way to keep him. But, hey, it works sometimes.

Alert

Just make sure not to cross the line! A Scorpio, in vengeance, will do the same back to you. And who can resist a Scorpio's sexy, stunning charms? Be careful not to make Scorpio too jealous—his pride may just outweigh his need for you.

The Little Stuff Counts

Scorpio, normally, is pretty informal. Although he can dress up at a moment's notice, he usually prefers to dress comfortably. However, he won't mind how you dress and may not even notice. A Scorpio man, in particular, will be unduly impressed by the sight of a beautiful woman in a tight dress—tasteful and conservative, not tacky. On her side, a Scorpio woman will be drawn to a man with a pleasing scent. Actually, all Scorpios have very acute senses—except for hearing, which usually tends to be as bad as his other senses are good (although sometimes they just pretend not to hear you).

Essential

Though Scorpio's hearing isn't as sharp as his other senses, he is gifted with a silky, sultry voice—it's strangely sensual. Most Scorpios, too, like sexy voices. While on the phone or sitting right next to him, whisper something tantalizing into his ear. This will work.

Scorpio is also extremely subjective to touch and taste. Many Scorpio women and men are wonderful cooks once they get a little practice. Cook for him, and make sure the food has diverse tastes—combine salty, sweet, and spicy, for example. This is an aphrodisiac for Scorpio. Stroke his thigh and you probably won't get to finish your meal: Scorpio will have you in bed before you've had your last bite.

Pillow Talk: Signs in the Bedroom

All Scorpios are incredibly accomplished lovers. They have an innate sexual instinct, and their passion rides them. You'll feel like you're swept away with dark, alluring Scorpio. But she won't seduce you unless her mind is there. Try to get her to laugh at herself. Scorpio places too much importance, sometimes, on the little things. She gets wrapped up in details and fails to see the big picture.

The Secret Scorpio Man

The Scorpio man tends to get obsessed about things. It may be you in the beginning. But once he has you, the obsession will probably shift to his work. Work and livelihood is very important to the Scorpio man. His coworkers, most likely, think of him as a dedicated soul—difficult as he is. He's a perfectionist. When things don't go his way, he has a hard time dealing with it, fretting and pouting in his free time.

This little tidbit is important to know because it may spill into your sex and relationship time together. Once you relax Scorpio sufficiently, though, he will pour his passion and dedication into you. His perfectionism, in this case, is directed to an entirely different goal. He'll want to seduce you completely and utterly. Here's one thing you don't have to worry about: Though the Scorpio man can dominate in bed, he won't mind letting you take the reins once in a while. It depends on his mood. The key to success in the bedroom with Scorpio is to follow his lead.

The Secret Scorpio Woman

Though she's outgoing, funny, and smart, she's got a lot going on under the surface. She seems so open and liberal with her feelings; instead, she has lots of personal issues that secretly haunt her. Whether these problems have to do with her relationship, her family, or her work, she'll entrust her skeletons to one person and one person only: her other half, her love. In other words, you'll know whether she loves you and trusts you—for Scorpio, it's if she confesses her deepest, darkest secrets.

 Fact

The Scorpio woman is also sensual. Though she may come off as conservative in public, she's passionate and playful in bed. She loves to be in love. She'll worship you with her actions more than words, but once you have her heart, you have a loving soul who would bring you the moon if she could.

But Scorpio woman is, indeed, a private soul. She can be coerced to talk more freely in bed. After making love, she lets her guard down. This is a perfect time to find her demons and get her to open up. For Scorpio, sex is like air—she needs it to breathe.

Sun Love Matches

Scorpio men and women are very instinctive. Unfortunately, they sometimes ignore this instinct in friendship and in love. With friends, they may keep relations going even if the bond isn't there anymore (mostly if the rapport is important for work contacts or social means). Plus, they're loyal to old friends. Also, sex can sway them greatly in love. If a mate is not right for them, they'll know it, but they'll stay if things are powerful in the bedroom. However, when Scorpios are truly in love, they'll let you know. You'll be their world. Scorpios usually go well with Water and Fire, the other "feeling" signs. And a female Scorpio is known for taking up with a Taurus man. Read on to discover the love combinations for the Scorpio woman.

Scorpio Man

These two go together so well that it's a little scary. However, the perfect, happy couple they appear to be in public is sometimes different from what they experience alone at home. The Scorpio man is possessive. Instinctively, he needs her to need him. He may criticize just a little too much, even get a little verbally abusive with her specifically (watch out!), but in bed, the fireworks are hot and heavy. If the Scorpio woman can let the Scorpio man feel like he's in charge, this can be a probable long-term relationship. The two also have an excellent chance for marriage. However, if there's any kind of abuse there (emotional or otherwise), it is highly recommended that this partnership be left to the wayside.

🅴❗ Alert

The Scorpio man is so crazy about the Scorpio woman that he tries to control her. In fact, he puts her down sometimes simply to keep her close to him. He doesn't want her to go too far out of his reach.

Sagittarius Man

The Sagittarius man is a lot more direct and blunt than the Scorpio woman, and the one thing he wants from her is the truth. She gives it to him as much as she can but has a hard time unmasking herself. However, if the Archer is patient, Scorpio will reveal all her hidden mysteries and will get to the point where she's completely direct with him. He never minces words. In fact, he has no filter. These two go well together, even though keeping the conversations going could be an issue from the get-go. They resolve it: It's her. In bed, Sagittarius has all the right moves if he doesn't doubt himself too much. All in all, though, this can be a fiery, passionate union. It is a very possible long-term relationship and also a great chance for marriage.

✅ Fact

The Sagittarius man needs to trust his feelings and go with it. If he's looking for too much assurance in the beginning, he may not get it from the Scorpio woman. He must give her time to open up for this love combo to work!

Capricorn Man

In the beginning, the Capricorn man will capture Scorpio's attention. She's drawn to his stability, to his friendly, easygoing manner—and to his looks. But the Capricorn man has other things on his agenda. He has trouble figuring her out, and this bothers him. He'd like things to go more smoothly. She'd like him to be more affectionate. He'd like her to be more apparent and earthy. This match truly depends on what Capricorn has in the rest of his chart. If his Venus is in a Water or even a Fire sign, they may have a chance. Perhaps this can be a possible long-term relationship. It's also a possible marriage, but not a likely one.

Aquarius Man

The Aquarius man is fascinated by the strange, the unpredictable. If the Scorpio woman can give him the freedom to roam, he might even fall for her. Chances are, though, he'd like to let the relationship go with the flow, and she wants promises right away. In bed, the Scorpio woman loves that nothing shocks Aquarius. She can be as free as she wants, and, though she may hold back, she likes the security of knowing that nothing is taboo—except emotional surrender. (Aquarians are notoriously distant in this respect.) This is a possible long-term relationship, but it's not a probable marriage. Again, though, only the two people involved can decide that.

Pisces Man

Love and sex isn't rocket science, and Scorpio wishes the Pisces man would understand this. Sometimes they misinterpret each other. She wants to make things simpler, and Pisces gives the Scorpio woman the kind of affection and devotion she's looking for. Pisces doesn't mind so much that she's possessive of him. In fact, he kind of likes it. They both like to touch, and the sensuality in this union can be deep and powerful. If Scorpio can adjust to Pisces's schedule—he has more energy than she does—this can be a good long-term relationship, even a very possible marriage. If Pisces doesn't get distant or even disassociated, it can work.

Question

How does Scorpio seduce Pisces?
With mystery. Pisces loves to solve a puzzle. The intrigue will keep him coming back for more. He also loves music and romantic settings.

Aries Man

Cool, sexy, dominant Aries completely fascinates the Scorpio woman. In return, she intrigues him. Unfortunately, Scorpio can try to hold Aries back when it comes to his socializing. This can be disastrous since he needs to feel free. Once he has the option to roam, he'll most likely run back to her side. Also, Scorpio may have trouble respecting the Aries man's rough and undiplomatic tactics. If that's true, the romance could be in trouble. In bed, they're both instinctive and can give each other the perfect dose of loving. If Scorpio is willing to let Aries shine, whine, and grumble—loudly—this can be a probable long-term relationship with marriage a possibility in the long run.

Taurus Man

Normally Earth and Water signs don't mix very well. But something else is at work here with Taurus and Scorpio. They're both sensitive, and they can both be traditional (though this is more likely of Taurus). Sexually, they're the two hottest signs of the zodiac. Scorpio is more instinctive and sexual, while Taurus is more sensual. If the Scorpio woman can take it slow and let Taurus lead, they will have no problems in bed. On the contrary, if the sex is no good, these two will not last. Out of the bedroom, Scorpio subtly steers the two. Strangely, this is known to be one of the best matches in the zodiac. Go figure: They just balance each other well somehow. This can be a possible long-term relationship and a possible marriage after that—even a great one.

 Alert

Watch out! Both Scorpio and Taurus have an obsessive side. In this case, Taurus might idealize and fantasize about the Scorpio woman, putting her on a pedestal that she may or may not deserve. However, this may just add to the strength of the relationship in the long run.

Gemini Man

The Scorpio woman is not likely to get a word in edge-wise with the Gemini man. There will be plenty of laughing. Though he'll capture her attention for brief stretches of time, she knows better than to wait for more. The Gemini man won't necessarily put in the time to break down her barriers and get to know the real woman behind the façade. And deep down, that's really what she's hoping for in a long-term mate: acknowledgment and acceptance. In bed, the Gemini man confuses the Scorpio woman with his role-playing and mumbling about "what he's going to do with her." "Just do it already," she thinks. In the long run, this can be a positive long-term relationship, but it's not a recommended marriage, unless the two can't get enough of each other. They're more likely to get tangled up in it because they just can't stop trying to figure the other one out.

Cancer Man

These two inflame each other across the board, spiritually, mentally, and even physically. Though Cancer probably needs more security than Scorpio does—even in the beginning—she can keep a Cancer man happy in almost all regards. Both are notorious game players, and the Cancer man can be quite the Casanova at times. The Scorpio woman, though, is intense enough to keep his attention. The only problem in this match is the way these two fight: She may think he's pretty immature at times. They go all out and bare their souls—without thought of the consequences of saying what first comes to mind. As a result, they can get nasty with each other, and the two have trouble forgiving afterward. In the end, however, this can be a very good long-term relationship, with a decent chance for marriage.

Fact

> The Cancer man just loves provoking the Scorpio woman to the point of hysteria. Her passion and anger is what he's after—he lives for the challenge of calming her and making her his own. This (not surprisingly) doesn't fly well with the Scorpio woman.

Leo Man

The Leo man simply can't figure out what to do with the Scorpio woman. She misinterprets and misunderstands what he does (in the beginning)—and he's pretty direct. He adores her and makes her know it by teasing, flirting, and romancing her. But she doesn't trust him. He's affectionate with many. No matter. After she goes to bed with him, she doesn't care if it's short or long term—she barely remembers her name. This is what will make Leo fall for her: her all-in attitude. The Leo man and the Scorpio woman in bed make a fantastic pair. When they get closer, too, they have passionate, sexy trysts and can laugh a lot together. If Scorpio can side with Leo when he complains (or goes on a verbal rampage) and also lay down the law with him, this can be a possible long-term relationship and also an excellent marriage.

Virgo Man

Virgo and Scorpio are like night and day. In fact, they're more likely to talk about and analyze their relationship together than they are to have one. Though Scorpio doesn't let on, she'd like just a little more attention and affection than the Virgo man is likely to give (by nature). Scorpio may have more worldly and glamorous tastes than Virgo. If Virgo has a lot of Water or Fire in his chart, they could get along well. Oddly, the two are both fascinated with dark or twisted humor—and may find close comfort in similar things they deem amusing (that others wouldn't). Still, this is probably not a long-term relationship, and it's an unlikely marriage as well, unless they somehow strike the right harmony together. Then, anything's possible.

Libra Man

Libra's occasionally distant emotional nature intrigues Scorpio, but he makes her wary, too. She gets insecure if he criticizes her, and she senses that she will never live up to his perfectionist ideals. To Libra, mysterious, sensual Scorpio is a real handful, and he's not quite sure if he's ready to deal with her expansive ways. A good roll in the hay will change his mind, if he's willing. But Libra is picky with his bed partners. He teases but only sometimes follows through, running hot and cold emotionally as well as physically. If Libra doesn't scare Scorpio off with his indecisiveness and commits fully to her, this can be a possible long-term relationship. It's also a possible, though not probable, marriage. Even when the odds are stacked against them, there are always those couples who come out winners.

Love Planets: Venus and Mercury

Scorpio in the rest of your chart always adds a bit of mystery, intrigue, and even sensuality. Scorpios are always intense and passionate. They also know how to capture the attention and affection of the opposite sex—without really trying. They're not flirtatious like aggressive Gemini. They're more laid-back: "I'm here. I'm it. I'm cool." And your Venus, or even Mercury, will add that extra "oomph" to your personality. Below, compare the other aspects in Scorpio.

Venus in Scorpio

Once again, sex is extremely important to you. Though you may even equate love with great lovemaking, you'll want all experiences you share with a mate to be intense and passionate. You can't help being possessive and jealous at times. Venus in Scorpio has an addictive side, too. Not just in terms of love— also to alcohol, perhaps, nicotine, or even antidepressants. Self-pity could be your biggest downfall. When you're in love and feeling happy, though, your mood and good nature are contagious. Venus in Scorpio goes well with Venus in Virgo, Scorpio, Pisces, Sagittarius, and Taurus.

Mercury in Scorpio

You truly care what other people think and that's good (mostly). You're instinctive and somehow know how to turn a conversation to your advantage. Charm is your middle name. When you speak, people listen. In fact, you may even have a sexy, sultry, or interesting voice. You may like one-on-one talks rather than big groups and chatting with many different people. A romantic dinner with someone you love, for example, could be an ideal evening for you. You definitely like to engage in deep conversations concerning people you love, politics, and the world. Mercury in Scorpio pairs with Mercury in Cancer, Scorpio, Leo, Taurus, and Sagittarius.

CHAPTER 9

Sagittarius

Sagittarius has two sides: one serious . . . and one that's extremely playful. He can seem like one person and then change his character entirely. These aren't moods—this is him. How do you get to the heart of Sagittarius? What do you do to win him? In this chapter, find out.

Are You "The One" for the Archer?

1. **Most Sagittarians, when taking an ideal trip, would chose:**
   A. Something low-key
   B. An adventure
   C. A trek to see the family
   D. A place close by for the day

2. **If Sagittarius gets angry at you, what should you do?**
   A. Walk away
   B. Fight!
   C. Change the subject
   D. Talk it out

3. **After the honeymoon period with the Sagittarius man, what will he choose first (given the opportunity)?**
   A. Family
   B. Hobbies
   C. Work
   D. Meeting with friends

4. **When a Sagittarian keeps bringing up a topic that's very important to her, she really wants you to:**
   A. Fight with her
   B. Agree with her
   C. Tell her to stop talking about it
   D. Make jokes about it

5. **What on this list would be a deal breaker for Sagittarius?**
   A. Lying about something
   B. Being nasty to Sag's family
   C. Cheating romantically
   D. Looking into Sag's private things

6. **When Sagittarius is part of a couple, who makes decisions?**
   A. Sagittarius likes to do it.
   B. Sagittarius likes the partner to do it.
   C. Sagittarius likes to share in the decision-making.
   D. Sagittarius listens but then blows it off.

7. **Which of these qualities is not a Sagittarius trait?**
   A. Honest
   B. Direct
   C. Manipulative
   D. Kind

8. **How do Sagittarians deal with a challenge, dating-wise?**
   A. They'll put themselves out there and rise up to meet it.
   B. They can't cope with the stress.
   C. They won't bother at all.
   D. They'll try once but—without a good response—they'll give up.

9. **What is often a deal breaker when it comes to relationships with Sagittarius?**
   A. They're not funny: Sense of humor is a problem.
   B. They're too sweet: They don't know when to hold back.
   C. They're self-absorbed: They like to be the center of attention.
   D. They're too honest: They say what comes to mind sometimes, not thinking of the consequences.

10. **If Sagittarius is at the brink of falling in love, he will most likely:**
    A. Profess his love with words
    B. Shower you with gifts
    C. Mess up to see if he can win you back
    D. Show you with actions

Answers: 1. b, 2. c, 3. b, 4. b, 5. c, 6. c, 7. c, 8. a, 9. d, 10. d

The Renaissance Man (or Woman)

For Sagittarius, learning something new is like breathing. She craves adventure and intense experiences. But here's the paradox. She may want to skydive, sail, learn foreign languages, and conquer new worlds, yet all the while she's looking for a partner who's something of an opposing force—one who will balance her out. In other words, Sagittarius wants to shine, and she needs someone who'll let her, who'll come along for the ride of a lifetime. The perfect Sagittarius partner has to be a tough cookie, laugh at all her jokes, and have fun with her. For Sagittarius, a boring life with her work or with a love partner is like not living at all.

ⓔ Essential

If you want to get Sagittarius's attention, listen. If she feels like you're yessing her to get out of the conversation, she'll get annoyed. Hear Sagittarius when she speaks—she has a lot to say!

In fact, Sagittarius has absolutely no patience with people who just don't "get it." She can be intolerant to the point of disgust if she believes someone is going about something "the wrong way." For Sagittarius, in fact, there's only one right way: her way. If you're a Fire sign or an Air sign, make sure to give Sagittarius her due. If you argue with her, she'll never see your side; she'll only think of you as a troublemaker. If you want to be with Sagittarius, let her think she's in control (even when she's not and knows it). Sagittarius—man or woman—needs to be heard and understood.

R-E-S-P-E-C-T

For Sagittarius, it's essential that his authority is respected and acknowledged. In important moments, it will infuriate him if you joke or fail to take a situation seriously. It's almost as if he was born with a chip on his shoulder when it comes to being given consideration. He also has a secret violent streak that can come out unexpectedly. Do yourself a favor and always make Sagittarius feel like a treasure.

 Fact

When Sagittarius starts criticizing you, just remember that he's his own worst critic, too. These rules don't apply only to you. They apply to him as well. In fact, he'll tell you his faults even before you discover them yourself. Though Sagittarius is a teddy bear, sweet and sensitive with the person he loves, he has absolutely no tact. He'll give it to you straight. He says the first thing that comes to mind—and we all know how much trouble this causes. No matter. When Sagittarius is really in love, you'll know it. He'll tell you, and you can believe him completely. Sagittarius never says he's in love if he's not.

Did we say treasure? Are you ready for this? Sagittarius is one of the most fun, interesting, talented, ironical signs of the zodiac. He has a knack for being good at everything he does. One minute he's telling you that he's an awful dancer; the next, he's sweeping you off your feet. Why? Kind, fun, and sexy as he is, Sagittarius is modest. He'll be the first to say that he's not that great—when you know that the exact opposite is true. He has two main motives: He likes compliments, and he's a perfectionist.

The Art of Attraction

Sagittarius likes to do exactly the opposite of what she's told. If you pressure or (heaven forbid) try to manipulate her in some way, she'll smell you out in a second—and she won't like it, not one bit. But don't worry about giving Sagittarius a challenge. She's built for it. In fact, Sagittarius likes to work a little for love. If she gets what she wants too easily, it's not going to hold her attention for more than a second. However, once the relationship starts, Sagittarius wants things to go smoothly. If the personal rapport is not working out, or Sagittarius feels the two of you have different ways of handling things, Sagittarius will be out the door before you can yell "Wait!"

Question

What's a good way to know if Sagittarius is in love?
Ask her. She'll tell you. Sagittarius isn't big on flowery words of love and devotion, but if her feelings are intense and sincere, she'll show you through action—and tell you, too.

The Long Haul

Sagittarius is not as independent as she seems. She instinctively knows whom to trust, and she likes good company. Though she seems just fine by herself, she lives to have a strong, wonderful companion by her side. Like all Fire signs, Sagittarius is an idealist and a perfectionist. She will not "settle" when it comes to love. Ironically enough, Sagittarius can be either the biggest player in the zodiac or the most devoted, loyal partner.

Sagittarius honors her commitments, and her word is as good as gold.

The Little Stuff Counts

How should you dress for a Sagittarius? Sagittarius doesn't like showy, ostentatious dressers. She's more likely to notice your smile or your eyes before the color of the shirt or brand of jeans you're wearing. Here's a tip, though: If Sagittarius is on a cusp bordering with Capricorn, she'll be slightly opportunistic. You can impress her by dropping names, telling her you travel a lot, or letting on that you have a close friend with a sailboat and a villa by the sea. (This works if she has Capricorn in her chart, too.) On the other hand, most Sagittarius men are impressed with knowledge of languages, foreign cultures, music, good wine, and any kind of ethnic food.

 Fact

Though every Sagittarius has a spiritual side, this sign is the least likely to believe in astrology, destiny, or even religion. If you ask someone their sign and they say, "I don't believe in it," nine out of ten times, you've stumbled on a Sagittarius!

Don't expect Sagittarius to fall to her knees and tell you she worships the ground you walk on. Sagittarius speaks ten times more with action than with words. Though she can talk about anything, something gets her tongue when it comes to romantic words of love. A mate of a Sagittarius who comes to accept this will be very satisfied, though. Whatever she does say will mean much more than the same thing from someone who throws compliments around to everyone.

Pillow Talk: Signs in the Bedroom

Sagittarius cannot resist a real challenge. For love, it's got to be there. For sex, this goes double. And don't even think of playing hard to get in the beginning and then letting him have your heart and soul. Real love mates of Sagittarius know that continuing the flirtation throughout their life together means issuing a challenge and letting him "come and get it."

The Secret Sagittarius Man

Sagittarius is one of the most macho signs of the zodiac. If you tell him he can't do something, he'll do it just for the sake of proving himself. You want to get Sagittarius into bed? Tell him he can't have you, and he'll stop at nothing to show you who's boss. The Sagittarius man can also appear emotionally distant. Don't let it fool you. He's passionate, clever, instinctive, and very sexual. In bed, let Sagittarius lead.

He can definitely, however, keep sex and love on different planes, so watch out! Again, ask him what he's after: He'll tell you. But insult a Sagittarius man on his lovemaking or his intelligence, and you'll never see him again. And, when it comes down to it, he's a realist. No matter how in love he is, he's not a slave to his passions (or a masochist) like some other signs—Taurus or Virgo, for example.

The Secret Sagittarius Woman

She's all woman. She knows herself well and knows her limits. She's not afraid of love or the emotions that go with it. She's all fire and passion, and she's a great friend, lover, and confidante. But don't be fooled. She'll let herself be conquered only if she wants to be. How do you spark a Sagittarius woman's interest? Here are a few tips:

- Don't play hard to get. Be hard to get (in the beginning . . .).
- Never talk about things you're not sure about. Instead, ask her to tell you about them.
- Listen to her.
- Be honest.
- Be modest, but charming.
- Always be a gentleman and treat her with respect.
- Don't be a pushover. Stand up for yourself.
- Make her laugh and make sure you laugh at her jokes.
- Show her you have a life outside of her.
- Talk in front of her to friends about how wonderful she is.

Above all, don't fawn all over the Sagittarius woman. She won't trust you or like you for it, and she certainly won't go to bed with you. Sagittarius doesn't mind a little public display of attection if she's into you. If she's not, she'll be cool as a cucumber. Though the Sagittarius woman is never haughty, and never a snob, even if she's nice to you, it doesn't mean she's in love with you. In bed, go by instinct. There'll be time for wild, uncensored sex and also time to make it slow and dreamy. In bed, too, the Sagittarius lady is more likely to say how she feels about you. Make sure you let her know how you feel as well.

 **Essential**

Both Sagittarius men and women have one true defect that you'll just have to accept if you want to be with them: timing in social situations. They're likely to say the wrong thing to the wrong person. Reason: They're candid, open, and honest . . . to a fault.

Sun Love Matches

Passionate, sexy, fierce, and even a bit dangerous, Sagittarius is potent and will look for a partner who's potent as well. Just keep in mind that Sagittarius likes to be the ruler. If he gets involved with bossy Leo or demanding Aries, it can work because the fire is there . . . but only if he's given his respect and his due. Authority is everything to Sagittarius. Sagittarius goes well with Water signs, too, who seem to balance him out. They also dote and give him the security and stability he secretly longs for. Read on to learn about the love compatibility matches for a Sagittarius woman.

Sagittarius Man

These two really know how to have a good time together. They're passionate about all the same things, and if there's one little thing they don't agree on, they understand how to give each other the time and space required to get over it.

 Fact

There are only two BIG problems with the match between the Sagittarius man and woman: the fighting and the making up. For one, neither Sagittarius will back down in a fight. Making up becomes a problem when Sagittarius craves a soft, stable, nurturing hand to turn to when he's willing to be coaxed.

They both know how to play, to love, and to make love. They have to be careful not to step on each other's toes, though. This can be a good long-term relationship and a possible marriage, although the balance here may be awkward and trying.

Capricorn Man

There is definitely something that inspires the Sagittarius woman's interest in the Capricorn man. He's intelligent, interesting, stable, and pretty much knows what he wants. Strangely enough, too, he exposes her sensitive side—something she doesn't show to many. In this case, though, it makes her feel oddly vulnerable. In fact, these two are cut from different cloths. The Sagittarius woman feels and goes with instinct, while the Capricorn man rationalizes. In bed, he normally does not have the fire or the passion to fill her with the emotions she craves. This is a possible long-term relationship, but it's not a probable marriage . . . although you never know what's written in the stars.

Aquarius Man

Aquarius and Sagittarius are strangely drawn to each other. The chemistry here can be powerful and wicked. Know one thing, though. Life isn't fair. Sexually, the two reach new heights. Emotionally and mentally, however, these two will eventually have big problems. Aquarius analyzes and thinks. Sagittarius wants affection, though she won't ask for it.

Ironically enough, this can be a very promising long-term relationship, but it's not necessarily a long-lasting marriage match—unless they can figure out something unique that actually works.

 **Essential**

They can travel together and have new experiences, but the Sagittarius woman will soon regard the Aquarius man as emotionally distant at times. True, these two are some of the more independent and liberal of the signs. But their common ground may stop there.

Pisces Man

Others see these two as complete opposites. She can be even more of a bully than he is (at times), yet still very feminine—nurturing, romantic—and sophisticated. In other words, she's a strong woman. For this reason, he gives her the respect and the power she craves. Therefore, this may be a good match.

True, if he has no Fire in his chart, he may be a little too sweet for her in bed. But if she's smart (which she is) and cares, she can bring out the reckless, stronger side of Pisces. He may not be the kind of he-man she's looking for (to dominate her in certain ways); however, if he decides to be loyal to her and has some fire in him, this can be a long-term relationship. It's also a very possible marriage (and a good one at that with the right match).

 Fact

The Sagittarius *man* and the Pisces *woman* is the ultimate combination. But the Sagittarius woman and the Pisces man may work, too. Quiet strength between these two is the ultimate factor. And they seem to bring out the best in each other.

Aries Man

Fire. Fire. Fire. The Aries man tempts the Sagittarius woman like crazy. He's got her (for now at least), and she knows it, even if she doesn't let on. She loves his unpredictability, his nerve, his sex appeal, and the fact that he's outright ballsy. She admires him for the way he deals with people. Unfortunately, when she gets to understand him better, she sees him as a showoff, a braggart, insecure, and someone who doesn't necessarily keep his word. They like to experiment in bed, and Aries will make Sagittarius feel completely cherished. This alone will get her, though she may suffer some disappointment in the future when his interests quickly turn off and on again. Most likely, she's more evolved and mature than he is. This pair can still be possible—for a long-term relationship or for marriage. Just make sure to read the fine print; know what you're getting into.

Taurus Man

The Taurus man sparks the Sagittarius woman's interest because she really likes the way he looks—well-built, sexy, and powerful. She's instinctively drawn to him sexually, and these two can move mountains in bed. The Taurus man pays homage to Sagittarius. He worships her, and she, in turn, knows what a treasure she's found. Unfortunately, Sagittarius may be too liberal and independent for some Taurus men. He'll want security and trust—so will she—but most likely, he'll be foolhardy about it. He'll mess up by trying to make her jealous thinking it'll work: It won't. If Taurus gets totally obsessed with Sagittarius, which he's prone to do, she may give him a chance. This can be a possible long-term relationship. It's also a possible marriage—and can be good if Taurus is emotionally mature and the two can synch up their communication styles.

🚨 Alert

Taurus will shy away from conflict, and when the two argue, he misses (or pretends to miss) the crux of the matter, the subtleties. This can drive the Sagittarius woman up the wall. If he's mature and honest, this can be remedied.

Gemini Man

Gemini makes Sagittarius smile and laugh. In fact, he also makes her feel . . . deeply. And this is a problem. Though Gemini appears sensitive and sensuous, he's really not half as emotionally driven as the Sagittarius woman. This is dangerous. She wants to conquer him—to make him feel. In bed, Gemini brings out the wildness of Sagittarius. She wishes they truly connected more. Strangely, these two are drawn together. This can be a very possible long-term relationship, but it's not a recommended marriage . . . though it's definitely been done before.

Cancer Man

This is a tossup. It really depends how mature the Cancer man is. If he knows himself and can voice his emotions, this can work. The Cancer man can sometimes gain security by playing the Casanova with women. But when he sees the Sagittarius woman, he gets inspired. He wants to win her, and she just may let him. In bed, they become incredibly adventurous if Sagittarius can make him think he's completely in charge. Remember, he's a Cardinal sign (meaning he likes to dominate.) No matter: She's instinctive enough to let him take the reins. This relationship can flourish only if Sagittarius gets to the bottom of who Cancer really is. He'll sidestep and hide from her scrutinizing gaze. If he lets her in, though, and if he's truly ready to settle down, this can be a good long-term relationship. It can be a good marriage, too, if the Cancer man has worked out all of his aggression and/or control issues.

Leo Man

Ouch. These two have a hard time getting together. Why? Believe it or not, their sexual craving for each other is so strong that talk is pretty much impossible. Also, both have a quiet side, with each failing to voice how they truly feel. The Sagittarius woman thinks the Leo man is just toying with her, but this may be simply an act. They misinterpret and misunderstand. Most likely, Sagittarius will put it out there and wait for the Leo man to come back strong and steady with verbal cues. But he's action-oriented, like the Sagittarius woman. Also, Leo needs someone to calm him down when he gets riled up: Sag is fire. That's hard. In bed, Leo whispers endearments Sagittarius has wanted to hear her entire life. And the physical side of things is perfect. If they can be a team and back each other up, they can have a long, passionate relationship. This is a probable long-term relationship and a very possible marriage (if they can work it out).

Essential

There may be a big problem here. The Leo man needs to be put in his place in private but never, ever in public. Sag must learn to hold her tongue—she always says what she thinks (which can be humiliating to Leo). Leo doesn't stay unless he feels a mate has his back—always.

Virgo Man

The Sagittarius woman is completely taken aback by Virgo's freshness. His wit and self-mocking humor get to her. She likes it. She also understands his abrupt way of dealing with people—she does it sometimes, too. But, strangely enough, she can't stand his intolerance of so many things. Unfortunately, this leads to trouble in the bedroom. Sagittarius loses just a bit a respect for the Virgo man only because they have two completely different ways of seeing things. She sparks his interest in a physical way—but that's all. These two could have a long-term relationship, but it's not probable. Marriage isn't likely . . . although this pairing has seen the light of day—and has shined brightly, too.

Libra Man

Sagittarius has got it bad for Libra. She senses a troubled soul—one whom she can save. She's right about the first part. He may have problems, but she's not likely the one who can rescue him. Actually, Libra sees her as too brash and bold for his tastes. He'd like to match her step for step—for at least one night, but not much more than that. If he goes to bed with her, it can be all sparks, but Sagittarius may just wake up the next morning regretting their liaison—which Libra might do, too. These two are perfectly friendship-made, but they aren't love-bound. All in all, this may be an okay long-term relationship, but it's not a probable marriage. Again, it's been done, though—with only some complaints.

Scorpio Man

If the Sagittarius woman was looking for someone cool, a real challenge, she's finally met her match. Dark, mysterious, sexy Scorpio gets her going, and he's enthralled by her, too. When does she fall in love with the Scorpio man? After she goes to bed with him. They fit together perfectly. However, Scorpio is much more pessimistic than optimistic Sagittarius. He can bring her down with his moody ways. She also provokes him to defend himself—which he detests. But she makes him laugh. If Scorpio is mature and has his temper under control, though, this can work. It depends on how much the two are willing to give passion and love a real chance. If they are, this can be a very possible long-term relationship and a beautiful marriage beyond that.

Love Planets: Venus and Mercury

Even if all the signs in your chart are Earth or even Air, a bit of Sagittarius will still give you an expansive, generous, fun-loving side. Sagittarius can even make Taurus or Capricorn more liberal. Freedom to travel and learn new trades is an interest Sagittarius can't deny. And because Sagittarius is a Renaissance man (or woman), you'll probably be good at everything you pour your heart into. Needless to say, Sagittarius is a positive, fiery sign to have light up your chart. Read on to learn some of the aspects.

 Fact

Like Scorpio, Sagittarius has a bit of a dark side, too. If your Venus is in Sagittarius, you are likely to experience some self-pity. You also tend to be harsh in your judgment of others and scathingly self-critical. Try to relax and give yourself (and others) a break.

Venus in Sagittarius

You probably crave adventure; intense experiences; wild, passionate sex; and all-or-nothing love. Sexually charged, you recognize attraction and desire in an instant. In love, you usually get what you want, when you want it. Some may say you're irresistible. Before you commit yourself to a relationship, you need to be convinced. You'll never settle for something or someone less than what you think is right for you. In fact, when you're really in love, you give all—though you're not clingy or too possessive. When you're not, you're a heartbreaker. You're honest in relationships, generous, and more sensitive than you'd like others to see. Venus in Sagittarius pairs well with Venus in Leo, Sagittarius, Pisces, Scorpio, and Cancer.

Mercury in Sagittarius

You may switch subjects too rapidly for other people's tastes, but that's because so many different topics fascinate you. You especially love to talk about foreign cultures and countries, the subtleties of language, travel, adventure, sports—doing them, not watching—and the intricacies of love and sex. You're funny, and you like to laugh. You're faithful only when you're really in love. You don't get along with people unless they truly appreciate irony, sarcasm, or your particular brand of humor. If someone doesn't get you, you try to explain yourself, but you won't waste too much time doing it. Instead, you're off following more worthwhile pursuits. You're a natural-born flirt, but oddly enough, you connect extremely well with babies, children, even animals sometimes, more than you do with people. Mercury in Sagittarius links well with Mercury in Sagittarius, Leo, Gemini, Pisces, and Cancer.

CHAPTER 10

Capricorn

Capricorn is always a fascinating type and not so easy to know profoundly. In fact, you'll have to dig deep to get to the heart of Capricorn. Here are some tried-and-true tips about the real Capricorn. In this chapter, discover his whole reason for being . . . and find out his life's desires.

Can You Tether the Goat's Loyal Heart to Yours?

1. **Who are Capricorns most likely to side with in a popularly televised debate?**
   A. Mom's take on it
   B. A best friend's rant on it
   C. Themselves—they trust their own ideas
   D. A journalist's point of view

2. **What are Caps, most likely, not?**
   A. Very smart
   B. Ironic and funny
   C. Extremely authoritative
   D. Overly dramatic

3. **You come to Cap with an important problem that's been bothering you. To Capricorns, solutions are:**
   A. Pretty much black and white—there's only one solution.
   B. Difficult to come by—and they can ponder for hours on it.
   C. Your problem—they never give advice.
   D. Tricky—all scenarios need to be considered.

4. **Capricorn sometimes has a flaw:**
   A. Too sentimental
   B. Judgmental
   C. Fickle
   D. Needy

5. **When you first start dating Capricorn, what's an important thing to remember?**

    A. Be "the victim": Cap can't resist saving a wounded soul.

    B. If Cap asks you to do something, don't do it: Cap is wowed by someone who challenges her requests.

    C. Make a good first impression: Cap likes when you're honest and down-to-earth.

    D. Dress flashy: Cap likes when you wear something that gets some attention.

6. **Capricorn is completed devoted (either begrudgingly or happily) to:**

    A. Work

    B. The gym

    C. Family

    D. Hobbies

7. **Capricorn may put up with:**

    A. A needy person

    B. A "yes" person

    C. A liar

    D. A skeptic

8. **You're on a date, and Cap really seems to like you. How does he behave?**

    A. Being mostly silent, listening

    B. Getting involved in the conversation

    C. Drinking too much from nervousness

    D. Texting work under the table—he can't help it

9. **You're on a vacation in Barcelona. What will Capricorn truly want to see?**

    A. Museums

    B. Art galleries

    C. Where all the locals hang out

    D. All of the above

10. **If you're fighting all-out with Capricorn, what's a dirty tactic in warfare that he may use?**
   A. Accuse you of things you've never even done
   B. Call you nasty names—things he will never take back
   C. Bring up things you've done from the past if it supports his point
   D. A Capricorn doesn't have any dirty tactics—he usually fights fairly

The Strong, Silent One

Capricorn seems easy to figure out. True, she can be predictable on some points. But at other times, she'll come out and surprise you. One thing every Capricorn concedes is that she knows herself well. She has strong convictions about what she's looking for in a mate—in this, yes, she has clear ideas. But even Capricorn can be swayed.

 **Essential**

> Capricorns are ten times slyer than you'd imagine (and much more so than Virgo and Taurus, the other Earth signs). They'll put a kernel of an idea into your head and then watch, wait, and see what you do with it.

Capricorn likes to analyze and formulate. Without a plan, she feels bereft. In other words, she's not likely to "wing it." But Capricorn goes more for a specific character type with certain moral ideas than for a certain look or body type. In love, she'll want a strong, vivacious partner she can be proud of. In truth, she's no wallflower himself. She may hide behind her scruples and ideals, but she can also be a lot more easygoing than she looks. She's always got something to say, and she doesn't freely give her approval right off the bat. Instead, she'll hand you a rope and let you hang yourself with it.

The Orderly and Cautious Soul

Most Capricorns tend to be orderly, but get this: They categorize people as well. In other words, besides keeping their houses relatively spic-and-span, Capricorn desperately wants to label you, put you in a marked box, and stick you on the shelf along with other classified would-be mates. Truthfully, she's not okay simply getting to know a three-dimensional you. She's very cautious about giving her heart, and she's likely to stereotype you to some degree before you two even make it out of the starting gate. You're either this way or that. And once Capricorn has "figured you out," she's not likely to change her mind so quickly or to tailor her "hard-won" results.

True, this can be tedious or even offensive, but here's a little secret: If you say and do all the "right" things in the beginning, you'll have Capricorn convinced she knows you. And since she's not likely to change her mind quickly on how she perceives anything—remember, she's a cardinal sign (she likes being "right")—you need only act the part in the very beginning. And then you're free to be you! How does that sound? (Capricorns are instinctive, so if they like you from the start, there's usually a reason.)

Emotional Power

It's sad to see that Capricorn gets a bad reputation for being cold, though. He's anything but. The truth is that Capricorn will hold on to the reins until he knows he can trust you. He also wants to make sure you two are on the same page. Sure, he's not likely to dive into a love situation; if he does, nine times out of ten he has someone in the wings as an emotional backup. But when and if he decides it's you, you're likely to have his heart served to you on a silver, gold, or platinum platter.

The Inner Child

Inside of a Capricorn man lurks a little boy he doesn't like to show. You can bring this out in him. Make him laugh at himself and the world around him; say things that will impress him and he's likely to make you the goddess of his heart. He'll do anything to win and keep you. What needs to come across here is that you're not a capricious, whimsical, free-spirit type (who's likely to leave . . . and hang him out emotionally to dry). You never drop money too easily. (He'll prompt and poke you to admit that you are! Don't fall into this trap.)

Capricorn is always attracted to this breath of fresh air: For example, Capricorn is instinctively enamored by generous, expensive-tasted, big-hearted Leo, but he will intuitively fear this kind of person at the same time. In fact, he will do his best not to get too emotionally involved because he senses that the combo will not work. Why? He hates to fail. Will it? No. Not if you know how to put yourself in the best light and show off your greatest assets.

 Fact

Capricorn is definitely not stingy. However, he's also not necessarily the financial whiz that most astrologers make him out to be. That's okay. Even if his funds are sometimes modest, Capricorn is still likely to be interested in financial security.

The Critical Capricorn

Like Virgo, Capricorn almost always takes himself too seriously. He's self-mocking at times and deliberately critical. In fact, he's likely to father you, telling you what you need to do and how you need to do it. You can stand up to Capricorn, but don't defend yourself. You must make sure you let him know that yes, he's right, and that you will immediately make the appropriate changes. If you don't, Capricorn will think you have your own agenda—one that doesn't agree with his. He will never appreciate this about you the way other independent cardinal signs like Aries or Libra would. Capricorn needs to dominate— especially the Capricorn man. So let Capricorns in general think they're in charge, especially with money issues.

The Art of Attraction

Above all, Capricorn wants assurance—should she falter. She does want emotional security, but one stereotype is true: All Capricorns need to know their love partnerships are also covered financially at all times. What many astrologers fail to see, however, is that the buck literally stops here. It bears repeating that not every Capricorn is good at making mountains of money. She only really needs to know that things can be paid for. This, indeed, is incredibly important to her, even if Capricorn makes it seem like it's not.

The Long Haul

Yet, Capricorn devotes her love, heart and soul, when she's sure of you. She's very linked with family. Actually, Capricorn is a real provider—the Capricorn man, especially. He'll want to be the major breadwinner. In fact, he can be a bit adamant about living off the money he, and only he, makes.

Capricorn, regardless of whether she's close to her family, is not likely to move to a different country or even another county on a moment's notice. She tends to stay close to home base or at least will take the time to decide on a big move. Also, Capricorn will stick around even when a relationship is less than stellar. Sure, she'll complain to her friends and family and even warn you that she's on her way out, but it will take a lot just for her to walk away without looking back. This is true of all Capricorns. For the record, Capricorn hates the thought of perhaps "missing out" (and also typically can't stand teary goodbye scenes).

The Little Stuff Counts

Capricorn, it should be said, is almost always conservative in nature. She very much appreciates an out-there, gaudy, sensual, and sexy look, but she's also drawn to the tried-and-true: tailored pants or a pencil skirt with pearls and a dignified silk blouse; good (comfy but expensive) shoes are perfect. It just depends on where you'll be going.

Resourceful and Inspiring

There's something incredibly inspiring about Capricorn. Her personality is so polished, even if her clothes aren't always. She's smart—like an international sponge. She soaks up all kinds of information and spews it out on a moment's notice. She's incredibly resourceful, too. And she's got a big heart—for the pursuits and people she deems worthy.

e! Alert

Just make sure not to get on the wrong side of Capricorn. Quietly and carefully, she'll sneak up on you—instinctively knowing how to push your buttons. And she has a fantastic memory . . . she can reach back decades into her bottomless memory to find something to throw back at you.

In truth, you need only win a Capricorn's affection to see the fiery, beautiful, sweet soul lurking underneath. With friends and in love, the Capricorn woman and Capricorn man are equally unlikely to wear their hearts on their sleeves. But if they really respect you and dub you a "worthwhile cause," you may feel like royalty—because they'll treat you that way. They're more givers than takers, generous rather than parsimonious.

Pillow Talk: Signs in the Bedroom

Surprisingly enough, Capricorn doesn't mind some aggressiveness on your part—at least to get the ball rolling. In fact, he'll probably welcome it. But Capricorn isn't the verbal lover Gemini or Aries or even Sagittarius may be. Actually, he's more likely to joke just to break the tension (and for emotional protection) than to spew out words of love, passion, and dreams of forever after.

The Secret Capricorn Man

Capricorn man is a sought-after candidate for long-term commitment. He worships his family and works hard to take care of everyone around him. He also makes a fantastic father. Capricorn, in bed, can sometimes be a hard nut to crack—depending on the individual. He can hold back; it may even seem that he likes—no, favors—the traditional positions. But when he lets go, his tastes vary across the board. Capricorn men are the first to hide their more "out there" ideas of sex until they really feel comfortable with you. Even then, they may still choose concealment.

 **Essential**

Most Capricorn men are not big talkers after the act. Whatever you do, do not analyze or comment about the sex unless it's high praise for him! Capricorn is sensitive and thin-skinned when it comes to his masculine pride.

The Capricorn man may sometimes keep his sexual fantasies bottled up. You can get them out of him, perhaps, by acting shy or inexperienced (even if you're just role-playing). Try playing the virgin—Capricorn will eat it up. In this sense, a Virgo woman is actually a good choice for the Capricorn man (in bed). You can be seductive and aggressive to get him into bed, but once there, let Capricorn take over. Remember, he likes to dominate. He needs to feel like the he-man he is, the protector.

The Secret Capricorn Woman

Like her male counterpart, Capricorn woman is smart with a capital "S." She can be crafty, too. If she's got it in her mind that she's getting a man into bed, she won't have much trouble with it. If you want to seduce her, there are a few things you can do. Though these may seem stereotypical or over the top, they'll still work. In order to capture the Capricorn woman, assure her of at least four of the following six things:

- She comes before your friends.
- You understand the way the world works.
- You know people who can help her get ahead with her career and in life.
- You have sincere feelings for her.
- You're not the least bit stingy.
- You'll be there for her emotionally and financially.

This may make the Capricorn woman sound opportunistic or even a little superficial. She's not. She sincerely wants to feel a bond with you—and these things may help her feel more comfortable. From her sheer practical nature, these traits are important to her. Never lie about anything, though. Capricorn can't stand a liar. She's straightforward about herself, so you need to be, too.

Sun Love Matches

Here is what's important to all Capricorns: security, intelligence, a quick sense of humor, financial know-how, street smarts, mental stability (capricious folks need not apply), self-confidence, and the ability to give emotionally. Capricorn is always attracted to the breezy freshness of Air signs, but this is not always the best partner for him. Sometimes, yes. Romantically, he gets along well with Fire signs, though other Earth signs may have the same ideals in life. Read on to learn about the love matches for Capricorn woman.

Capricorn Man

These two have the same ideas about how things should be done. They know how to build a future together the "correct" way (according to their standards), and this seems to work. But a couple of problems come with this union. First, they beat each other to the punch line—since they think so alike, the surprise factor is ruled out. Also, when left alone in conversation, they can get as serious as a funeral. If one of them has many Air signs, this won't be a problem, though. Sexually, two Capricorns can be either soul mates in bed or partners who rub each other the wrong way (literally and figuratively). All in all, this relationship can be heavy—though it has worked for some. With Air signs in either of their charts, this can be a long-term relationship and a possible marriage. We won't discount it just yet.

 Fact

There are two types of Capricorns: the pessimist and the idealist. They're complete opposites. For a Capricorn union to work, two of the same types must come together. In this case, opposites do not attract.

Aquarius Man

It's such a shame these two have their differences. If they could solve them, they'd get along great. Chances are, the Capricorn woman will be the one to end it if it gets to the point of stay or go. Aquarius is intelligent, interesting, fun, and crazy about the Capricorn woman. But even so, the Aquarius man probably can't be what she needs and wants. He puts his friends before her. He has spending habits that drive the Capricorn woman mad. The truth is, though, there can be real love here. If these two can get it together, this can be a very possible long-term relationship. It's a possible marriage (even an excellent one) if Aquarius chooses to give Capricorn what she's looking for: devotion to her over a nutty social life with buddies or work contacts for him.

Pisces Man

Sorry to say, these two don't go together. There may be attraction, but that's where it probably ends. Pisces gets annoyed at Capricorn's know-it-all attitude. He admires her intelligence but wonders about her street smarts. Also, Capricorn can break Pisces's idealistic bubble. She's a troublemaker, he thinks, as he heads for the hills. Pisces is also sensitive to Capricorn's criticism, and he may just think she's not feminine enough for him. In bed, they can have an interesting liaison if he wows Capricorn sufficiently in all other areas. Then she'll let him dominate (for a minute). This is not a probable long-term relationship and not a likely marriage, either, unless this Pisces man is particularly strong—and Cap just "gets" him.

Aries Man

The Aries man has enough passion, fire, and stamina for the both of them. The Capricorn woman doesn't necessarily trust his jump-into-love ways, but she lets him woo her. Chances are, though, she may not have the patience Aries needs when he acts like a little boy. If Capricorn is not careful, she'll unwittingly insult him, and he'll change his mind about her quickly. In bed, this can be a fiery affair. If there's anyone who can open up Capricorn, it's Aries. This can be a possible long-term relationship. It's not a probable marriage, though not impossible. It'll just take tons of work—and if there's love there, anything can happen.

✱ Essential

Instinctively, the Capricorn woman doesn't believe Aries will be the secure rock she's looking for in life—and she's probably right. But he thrills her all the same.

Taurus Man

There's a sexual thing going on here, though, truthfully, Capricorn knows far too well how to get Taurus to do exactly as she wishes. This may ruin the fun for a Capricorn woman who wants to play, but it's a big turn-on for the Capricorn woman who's looking for a secure partner. When it comes to money, the Capricorn woman is the Bull's ultimate fantasy. Though he spends it in odd places (ones that she probably doesn't agree with), he's still mostly generous with her, and she appreciates that. This can be one hot sexual fling, but Capricorn may not trust Taurus's feelings for the long term. This can, however, be a possible long-term relationship, maybe even a good marriage, but they'd have to work for it.

Gemini Man

Of all the Air signs, this one is the least likely to bring out the best in the Capricorn woman. Although they can have a nice flirt together, they're likely to have little else in common beyond a good sense of humor and an attraction. Capricorn's brand of humor is a little more sarcastic, subtle, or ironic. Gemini amuses Capricorn, though. However, they can have fabulous sex and maybe even an affair that lasts—until one of them starts talking marriage. This can be a possible long-term relationship. It's also a slightly possible marriage if Gemini has tons of Earth in his chart (or is supergrounded)—but only if. It's been done with great success in rare cases.

Cancer Man

It's interesting. These two recognize the good within each other. In other words, they like each other as people. They can have conversations on everything (though Cancer may be seemingly more close-minded than even practical Capricorn—and that's only a bluff). Cancer, sometimes, may even enjoy provoking Capricorn—getting a reaction from her by making her angry. Capricorn is so cool, calm, and collected—sometimes. The two signs both prefer to have the upper hand. In bed, they take turns. In fact, this is probably the best thing in their relationship: wildness, fun, adventure, and even kinkiness (if Capricorn's willing) work in the sack. This is a possible long-term relationship and marriage—a tough thing . . . but up to them.

 Alert

When these two fight, get out of the way! Do not get involved in the kind of maneuvers they pull on each other. Each will try to get you to help them or find out information. One word: *don't.*

Leo Man

Leo and Capricorn can get along so well. Mentally, they're made for each other. The Capricorn woman inspires Leo to be the best he can be; meanwhile, she compliments him and strokes his ego. The one thing she doesn't understand about Leo is that he can be insecure at times. He's not as strong as he seems. She can also be insensitive to his feelings and overly critical at times. Leo admires Capricorn's sense of humor, intelligence, and all-around interesting personality. Truthfully, though, these two can have a hard time of it in bed. Both are too quiet for the other's tastes. Leo wants gushing words that Capricorn can't provide. He also wants more drama and fire in the bedroom, and Capricorn tends to stay away from drama. All in all, this can definitely be a long-term relationship and even a possible marriage. It can be excellent if the two "get" each other.

Virgo Man

Chances are, the Virgo man just doesn't give the kind of emotional attention the Capricorn woman needs and secretly hopes for. She may seem like a pessimist, but she genuinely wishes Virgo would turn around and worship the ground she walks on. When it comes to money, finances, starting up new businesses, and planning for the future, no one impresses Capricorn the way the Virgo man does. Sexually, Capricorn can feel when Virgo's holding back. She wonders why he's so secretive about his sexual habits. However, if Virgo is willing to open up and Capricorn is, too, it's a good long-term relationship with a good chance for marriage. If the two don't feel like something is missing, it can work.

Libra Man

Strangely enough, this can be a very positive union. Libra brings out Capricorn's fun, happy side, and, in turn, Capricorn gives Libra the kind of emotional security he's looking for. If she's a soft Capricorn, so much the better. Sexually, Libra can inspire Capricorn to try new things. Capricorn knows deep down she's always wanted to experiment, but she'll never let on. Therefore, Libra will feel like a master in the bedroom. This can work. However, it must be a strong Libra guy—full of conviction (not all are). It's a possible long-term relationship and also a possible marriage, depending on their willingness to compromise.

 Fact

Libra is a cardinal sign and wants to lead. Capricorn does, too, but if she's in love, she'll know how to handle him. (This will be difficult for the Libra man.)

Scorpio Man

Sexually, Scorpio knows how to get to Capricorn. Face it: He knows how to titillate anyone. Instinctively, Scorpio can feign innocence, all the while pulling out Capricorn's secrets without her knowing it. He's smart in this aspect, and hopefully he won't discover any skeletons he's not willing to deal with. The same is true of Capricorn. She'll dissect, analyze, and try to get to the heart of Scorpio. This actually may be a case of two wrongs not making a right because they're too similar at times. They're likely to have a very strong attraction. Therefore, this can be a possible long-term relationship, but it's not a recommended marriage. Again, it's up to the two of them.

Sagittarius Man

If Sagittarius is born closer to the Scorpio cusp or in the middle of Sagittarius and Capricorn, these two have less of a chance. A Sagittarius bordering Capricorn is likely to interest the Capricorn woman more. However, these two have truly different ways of operating. If a particular Sagittarius man needs more security than most others, though, the Capricorn woman can be a perfect match (especially if he has a love of money). Sexually, Capricorn recognizes Sagittarius for the talented lover he is, and Sagittarius's down-to-earth side feels a natural bond with Capricorn's earthy, sexual bent. If he's very attracted to her, he can win her love. If not, she may just go to bed with him simply for curiosity's sake. This can be a positive long-term relationship with a possible marriage in the future. However, this match wouldn't be an easy one.

Love Planets: Venus and Mercury

If you've got Capricorn in the rest of your chart, it will make you weigh out pluses and minuses before committing. When you make a pledge, though, you're more than likely to honor it. Venus in Capricorn, for example, tends to take love very seriously and is not likely to cheat on a partner. A certain inherent wisdom comes with the sign of Capricorn, too. Below, discover what Capricorn means to the rest of your personality.

Venus in Capricorn

Dedicated, loving, and loyal, Venus in Capricorn can be the most finicky in love. But when you commit, you're a wonderful partner. Though you may be extra critical of your mate, you do it out of love. Unfortunately, many partners aren't willing to accept this. A person needs to be thick-skinned to deal with the likes of you. You also change between being idealistic and practical, romantic and matter-of-fact. You're a tough nut to crack, and many wonder if they'll actually dig you all the way out of your shell. Venus in Capricorn goes well with Leo, Capricorn, Virgo, Libra, and (sometimes) Aquarius.

Mercury in Capricorn

A fast talker, that's what you are, but only when you feel like it. You can be wildly antisocial, at times. You always seem to find the one big interest of the person you're talking to. Though you have zero patience for ignorance and flights of fancy, you can amuse yourself talking with almost anyone—even if you can't dredge up an ounce of respect for the person. You don't even bother trying to be overly nice. Though you're not particularly nasty, it goes against your code of ethics to be fake to someone you don't like. Instead, you're more likely to say hello and then head the other way. It's important to you that people listen to what you're saying. Mercury in Capricorn goes well with Mercury in Capricorn, Libra, Leo, Taurus (maybe), Sagittarius, Virgo, and Aquarius.

CHAPTER 11

Aquarius

Remember the Broadway show or the hit movie Hair? Even if you don't, it's the "Age of Aquarius" we're talking about: freedom to be you and being loved for it . . . adoring the unusual, the contrary, the different, and even the offbeat. These are all real traits of the slippery Aquarius. How do you win his heart? Read on.

Can You Thrill Aquarius—Truly and Deeply?

1. **What is a good way to get Aquarius's attention?**
   A. Be sweet and complimentary
   B. Be different and independent
   C. Be chic and stylish
   D. Drop some famous names

2. **Aquarius is, in some ways, usually:**
   A. Annoying
   B. Obnoxious
   C. Spiritual
   D. Grounded

3. **Which girl will an Aquarius guy most likely go for?**
   A. The workaholic feminist
   B. The quirky writer or artist
   C. The conservative, straight-laced type
   D. The model type

4. **Aquarius is known to have a soft spot for:**
   A. People who cry to them
   B. The disabled
   C. The underdog
   D. The sick

5. **Aquarius's element is:**
   A. Fire
   B. Air
   C. Earth
   D. Water

6. **Aquarius needs to have _____ for a relationship to work.**
    A. Space
    B. Togetherness all the time
    C. Control
    D. Another person on the sidelines

7. **What's the ultimate surprise gift for an Aquarius woman?**
    A. Jewelry
    B. A weekend trip away for two
    C. A fur coat
    D. An invitation to a convention on health and beauty

8. **What is the one bad quality in a person that Aquarius probably couldn't manage?**
    A. Wildness
    B. Pettiness
    C. Outrageousness
    D. Damaged

9. **Whom would Aquarius talk to at a party?**
    A. The conservative Wall Street type
    B. The staff serving the food
    C. The creative musician type
    D. All of the above

10. **You propose some outrageous thing to do on a moment's notice for the weekend. Aquarius will probably:**
    A. Tell you you're nuts and continue on with the conversation
    B. Laugh and say, "Let's go. What time?"
    C. Debate back and forth whether or not you should go
    D. Get angry that you'd even propose such a thing . . . Aquarius doesn't do spontaneous

Answers: 1. b, 2. c, 3. b, 4. c, 5. b, 6. a, 7. b, 8. b, 9. d, 10. b

The Eclectic

Nine times out of ten, Aquarius will throw you for a loop. He seems so attentive, so interested, and so curious about you. You feel so special with him. Guess what? It's possible he's like this with everyone. But it's also possible you're the one . . . and you need to know the difference. Aquarius loves being entertained and amused. The world—including the people in it—is his oyster, and breaking people down is his art. Aquarius gets bored easily. He needs constant stimuli.

The Friendship Sign

Yes, this is the friendship sign. Yet, strangely enough, many astrologers fail to mention that Aquarius can be actively antisocial when he feels like it. This has more to do with the company than with how he feels about himself, though, which is what distinguishes Aquarius from other antisocial signs (like Scorpio or Cancer). If Aquarius even senses he'll have fun with you or a "different" kind of evening, he'll be dressed and out the door in a jiffy, ready for the night ahead.

 **Essential**

Aquarius has so many fans! They all relate to him in some way, and he's always nice to everyone. Therefore, he tends to attract undesirables—people with whom he wouldn't mind *not* being friends, but who will remain just acquaintances nevertheless.

Higher Beings

You're not likely to find an Aquarius who isn't spiritual. Even if she seems practical at heart, she still believes, if only a little (and actually more than she wants to), in a higher force—or destiny. The strange, the mystical, the odd and wonderful will always inspire Aquarius to dream a little dream.

❓ Question

Does Aquarius get attached?
Of course! It just takes more than sex, attraction, good conversation, and financial security to get them involved. Aquarians see the big picture. If you're part of their future, absolutely.

True, Aquarius has the power to emotionally distance herself more than any other sign. And she is able to control what she shows to others. Even if Aquarius is dying inside of love, she'll make light of it. What you see, then, is the product of someone who is very good at talking to and convincing herself.

The Art of Attraction

Just what is it that attracts Aquarius? He'll say, "I know it when I see it." In fact, the only constant in Aquarius's liaisons is that each partner is unique. Are you a showoff? Do you flaunt your money, car, or nice clothing? Aquarius couldn't care less. He goes for sure self-confidence, a quiet arrogance, and something or someone he's not sure of. Yes, Aquarius wants a bit of a challenge. But if you're too much of a challenge, he won't waste his time like a Fire sign would. Strike a balance.

The Long Haul

Though Aquarius can be very instinctive, he's actually the most naive of all the signs. Why? He trusts everyone. And he always roots for the person he believes is the underdog, even if that's not the true case at all. In other words, even if the "underdog" is snowing him under, Aquarius will quickly rise to the occasion and take this individual under his wing. For those who know semipractical Aquarius, it's hard to understand how he can be so gullible. Why doesn't he see through those preying on his good nature?

But Aquarius is always sought after, and for a reason. He doesn't have a set rule of conduct. Instead, each situation is new territory. He can make an excellent parent, one who shows his child acceptance no matter what.

 Question

Is Aquarius faithful?
Here's a simplified answer: only when he's really in love and can see a future with someone. If not, the answer is no, not ever. (The only possible exception is if he has his Venus in Capricorn.)

The Little Stuff Counts

Aquarius is not necessarily into glamour. He knows how to dress down, and he's far too practical to dress up for a barbecue. Actually, there is an androgynous theme that presents itself many times with Aquarius. Some Aquarius women are tomboys, and some Aquarius men have a feminine side. It depends on the person. But Aquarius likes to shock people. He does it for fun.

Sexiness Is What Counts

Aquarius looks for an innate sexiness in a love partner. It doesn't really matter how you dress, as long as you come off collected, grounded, and not clumsy in the least. Actually, Aquarian men usually go for a less conservative genre of dress (people, too)—though some women (and men) do like a bit more conservative dress for public outings. Aquarius women are attracted to masculine, he-man earthy types, and Aquarius men like natural, feminine types who wear little makeup. Don't even think of playing the traditional wife/husband. Aquarius has no use for you if you're just trying to impress or if you're typical or mundane.

Pillow Talk: Signs in the Bedroom

One word here: Grab! Aquarius is impressed by bold, outrageous moves. You can seduce her before you've even won her heart. Just keep in mind that Aquarius, more than any other sign in the zodiac, can absolutely separate love from sex. She will sleep with whomever, wherever, whenever she wants. No compunction, no regrets.

Essential

Aquarius never goes for shy partners. She instinctively looks for people who can dominate her. This is even true of Aquarius men . . . to a degree. Aquarius always needs to look up to a partner.

But sex is very important to Aquarius. You can make Aquarius fall in love in this way. She'll get used to you, addicted to you, if you see her over a period of time. This is an excellent way to sneak up on Aquarius. Before you know it, you'll have her. And she'll be yours, too.

The Secret Aquarius Man

Bright, lively, fascinating even, this man can get you to talk—and how! Here is where you need to be extra careful. The Aquarius man looks for a few things in a love mate. He'll be friendly and gregarious, but all the while, he's watching for warning signs. He knows what he doesn't want. Look at the following list. If you give Aquarius an idea that you are any of these things, he will run the other way:

- Needy
- Insecure
- A wallflower
- Neurotic in any way
- A hawk, in terms of your politics (Aquarius wants peace)
- Lacking a good group of friends
- Too possessive
- Not interested in traveling

Friends are important to the Aquarius man. If you try to rule his life, or tell him not to go out too much, he'll do exactly the opposite of what you say.

 Fact

The Aquarius man wants the world to be a better place. Show him you're interested in saving the planet, charity, animals, and/or starving children. He will need to know your ideals mirror his own.

Aquarians are born rebels. They live to go against the grain. They need to learn something new every day and can't stand to be bored. If you want an Aquarius man, let him win you. Show him you've got a life, a million things that interest you, and let him know you know how wonderful you are. He'll catch on.

The Secret Aquarius Woman

This woman has more fans than any of the other signs. People are drawn to her. Men are attracted to her. Why? She seems so down-to-earth, so tranquil and caring. In truth, she does empathize with almost anyone. Put Aquarius in a room full of people where she doesn't belong, and she'll still come out having every person in the place wanting to be her friend. She can rub shoulders with the lot of them. She's a chameleon. And she's no snob—not ever.

 Fact

The Aquarius woman *can* make love when she's not in love . . . she's just ten times more likely to "finish" when she is in love. Try as they do to go against the grain, Aquarian women, to their dismay, actually do need to be in love to experience good lovemaking.

What interests her? The weird, the strange, the unusual— that's what. Take her to an ethnic restaurant, preferably one where you can sit on the floor on cushions. Eye contact is very important here. Seduce her with deep, sensual, sexy stares. Always be yourself, though. Aquarius can smell a fake a mile away. Ask her what she wants—she'll tell you. Get her to open up, and she'll feel more connected to you. That's the secret. You'll have her.

Sun Love Matches

If Aquarius has learned one thing in life, it's that he likes the unpredictable. Aquarians, themselves, are the most spontaneous creatures. Aquarius lives to say things to shock you, and he changes on a dime just to confuse you. He hates it when someone tries to figure him out. On the same note, though, Aquarius is immediately attracted to sensual, thinking Earth signs who balance out his sometimes overly cool, tranquil demeanor. Other Air signs interest him as well, but only if the intended has a bit of Earth in her chart. Otherwise, the two never get around to doing anything. Read on to discover the love matches for the Aquarius woman.

Aquarius Man

This couple is wildfire. Each sets a match to the brush and waits to watch it explode. They egg each other on, provoking each other past a healthy limit. Actually, both are tranquil—at least, that's the appearance they create—and are simply waiting for the other to make a move. This can be a problem. They make each other jealous and ignore the big issues. To stay together, they need to confront the reality of the situation. Sexually, they're made for each other. If this is love, it can work. If it's not, these two will do more damage to each other than either imagined possible. All in all, the match is a positive long-term relationship and a very possible marriage.

Pisces Man

"Ah, a poet," the Aquarius woman thinks. But what she senses is the Water in him, something that she may lack herself. Strong feelings sometimes equal weakness for her. She's interested, though, in what he has to say. He's more powerful than she believes. If she gives him a chance, his strength will come out. In fact, he's just as crafty as she is.

 Fact

> There's something that probably doesn't click with Aquarius about Pisces. They're cut from different cloth. They like each other, but they don't necessarily trust each other.

Pisces will shy away from Aquarius in bed. She may be a handful for him. Maybe they can have a brief, fun fling. This is not a probable long-term relationship (but not a negative one, should it occur), and it's also not a probable marriage. Only the stars know.

Aries Man

This is a possible union. Here's the rub: The Aries man needs someone he can cuddle with. Though he's a strong he-man (which inevitably turns Aquarius on), he's also a big softie. Family is very important to Aries. He'll woo her and wow her at first with his wild, passionate declarations of love. But then he'll wonder if he can keep a real hold on her. She's not exactly begging to have children, settle down, and be his property. (The Aries man is notorious for putting women in their place.)

Still, this can work if the Aquarius woman is very in love with him. She knows how to get his attention and keep it. If she's a strong Aquarius woman and lays down the law for him, this can be a probable long-term relationship and marriage.

Taurus Man

This could be a great combination with the right two people. Taurus is sensuous and daring, and he makes Aquarius laugh. She's intrigued by his down-to-earth, no-nonsense approach to life. He's got everything on the ball, and he inspires her to do the same for herself. She also senses he can take good care of her. For some reason, he actually brings out her mothering nature. In bed, the two make fireworks. Sensual Taurus brings Aquarius to new heights. Ironically, Taurus can be very traditional, and Aquarius is not conventional in the least. Possessive Taurus, though, doesn't scare Aquarius one bit because he's not too clingy with her. He's independent, too, which is a good combination for Aquarius. This is a good chance for a long-term relationship, and there is a very good outlook for marriage . . . especially if Aquarius doesn't shock Taurus to the core (or try to rush him to the altar).

Gemini Man

Did we say "troublemakers"? Yes. These two cause confusion and chaos around them. The Gemini man can convince Aquarius to do almost anything. She's game. He'll instigate, though, and she'll be the one to carry it through.

Essential

Both Aquarius and Gemini like to shine, and Aquarius gets miffed if Gemini becomes a showoff or seemingly self-absorbed. If he is prone to tantrums or little lies, too, she will not stay to see the finale.

The Gemini man, however, is more wary about love with Aquarius than the other way around. He can be a little needier than she can, too. Though he amuses her, she's not at all sure she trusts him. Ditto for Gemini. This can work if both are mature and ready for something real. It's a possible long-term relationship, potentially leading to marriage. It's tough, though. Their bond must be strong and their ideals for the future the same.

Cancer Man

Cancer inspires Aquarius to be the best she can be. Her work flourishes with him. He supports her emotionally, all the way. They laugh together, and Cancer loves her self-mocking, droll sense of humor. He loves the fact that she's outgoing, but this bothers him, too. He seriously worries if he can control her—and he's soon to find out that maybe he can't. In fact, Aquarius is probably not capable of giving Cancer the kind of security he needs. Sexually, these two can be creative, spontaneous, and more than willing. However, although this relationship can make for a long-term relationship, it's not necessarily the best match for marriage. (Chances get better if Cancer is extremely secure with himself.)

✅ Fact

Aquarius and Cancer are very instinctive, but Cancer relies more on feeling and Aquarius rationalizes. This can be a problem when they fight. For things to work, Aquarius needs to trust Cancer and let him win—which will be hard for her.

Leo Man

It's hard to say what the attraction is here. In terms of chemistry, they're a powerful mix. Most likely, the Leo man will want to sexually attack the Aquarius woman right away. She stirs up something in him, and he'll need to show her how he feels—physically. Instead, she needs to talk to feel a connection. When Leo's quiet, she doesn't realize that he's shy or pensive. Instead, she imagines he's judging her. Leo is sometimes critical with Aquarius, it's true, and though it wouldn't bother anyone else, his perfect, precise style drives Aquarius nuts. Also, she needs to feel free. He secretly wants a loyal, faithful partner he can dominate. He'll find it difficult with her. This can be a long-term relationship, but it may not be a likely marriage . . . unless they meet at a time when both can strike a good balance.

Virgo Man

This may be a decent match with Aquarius, depending on the two. He amazes her with his business savvy. Aquarius, who's not necessarily interested in marrying a millionaire, is still interested in financial security. Virgo can provide her with this. She admires him for his ambition—probably because she sometimes lacks it herself—and is proud of his accomplishments and far-out money-making ideas. Virgo is very creative, both in work and in bed (once he lets go, anyway). His earthy sensuality awakens the sexual woman within. He also lets her do what she wants. The only problem here is that Virgo is antisocial and not always demonstrative. This can work, though. They have a good chance for a long-term relationship and a decent chance for marriage (but only if Virgo is more of a go-with-the-flow type).

Libra Man

Believe it or not, Libra actually has a bigger libido than even Aquarius. He'll have her craving him before she's realized what has happened. The problem in this case is indecision—a constant with Libra, but Aquarius brings it out in him more. He's not sure of her. She's not sure of him. They waver back and forth from being completely enamored to bickering like children.

Fortunately, Aquarius usually handles it with tact and directness (for the most part)—a lot better than, say, Gemini would. In bed, they talk, laugh, and furiously consume the oxygen around them, burning it up as they go. This can be a long-term relationship, leading to a possible marriage.

Essential

Libra hates to argue, but Aquarius challenges him, bringing everything out in the open, which is strange for Aquarius, who normally waits until the last second to make waves. She provokes Libra because she senses it bugs him.

Scorpio Man

Scorpio doesn't trust Aquarius much. Aquarius trusts Scorpio even less. But this only happens after some time together. In the beginning, they're like two peas in a pod. Aquarius knows how to handle moody Scorpio with her positive, breezy character. If anyone can pull him out of the doldrums, it's her. However, his stress weighs on her and sometimes affects her too much. It can be an unhealthy situation if Scorpio is not mentally balanced and/or somewhat spiritually evolved. The bedroom can be passionate and sexy if Aquarius isn't pushy. This is a possible long-term relationship, but it's not a probable marriage. One never knows.

Sagittarius Man

At first, Sagittarius can be attracted to Aquarius's eclectic style. They both love to travel, and they have tons to talk about. He also sees and senses the grounded part of her that not everyone notices. The fact that she's so interested in the world makes him like her. But love? Sagittarius is way more fiery and intoxicated by feelings than emotionally wary Aquarius. He wants to be nurtured and doted on, while she doesn't always have the patience. Instead, she expects him to service her—which he will do, at least for a while. Eventually, Sagittarius may come to believe that he can't rely on her to be grounded. Again, emotionally they may be on two separate planes. This can last for a little while. They may make a seemingly short- to long-term affair last for a while, but it's not a highly recommended marriage.

Capricorn Man

Of all the Earth signs for Aquarius, this one is the most interesting choice—and it depends on the man. It's impossible to generalize. Most Capricorns are conservative at heart and practical, but not all. The way some Aquarius women go on binges would make a practical Capricorn batty. She spends. She likes to go out. She socializes. In this case, Capricorn absolutely needs to have control of the wallet. Aquarius doesn't get this. She'll do what she feels like doing. He criticizes her, then she defends herself and gets angry. Not all Aquarius women are like this, however. Some are more grounded. This type will go better with Cap.

Capricorn doesn't open himself up enough in bed for her. She can bring it out of him, though, if she's willing to go slow. Mentally, they can get along, but Capricorn may be wary of Aquarius's strange tastes. He could think her superficial. All in all, this is a positive union. It could be a long-term relationship—definitely possible and actually wonderful for marriage, too . . . especially if it's the right match and the stars align for them.

Love Planets: Venus and Mercury

Aquarius is interested in anything and everything. A little Aquarius in your Venus and/or Mercury will instantly make you a curious cat. You'll want to understand how things work and why. This aspect also makes you friendly and eager to help people in situations less fortunate than your own. You trust easily—sometimes too much. Remember, Aquarius is a social sign. Even if your sun sign is a bit antisocial, Aquarius will always lighten up your personality. Read on for a more comprehensive outlook on this.

Venus in Aquarius

Sorry to say that this may be one of the least faithful love signs of the zodiac. There is only one way Venus in Aquarius can be true to a partner: when he or she is in utter love. Aside from that, you're able to separate yourself. Actually, you can't help it. But that doesn't bother you. Instead, it gives you the upper hand in every love relationship—because you're the challenge. Sex is very important to you. You need to feel loved completely before you can really let go in bed. Venus in Aquarius goes well with Venus in Taurus, Virgo, Capricorn, Aquarius, and Libra.

Mercury in Aquarius

You vary from being loquacious when you're interested in something to going silent when you're not. No one knows what's going to come out of your mouth. One thing, though, is that you're never vulgar. You have an inherent elegance that comes out in your speech, a basic goodness that's hard to deny. People want to talk to you and confide in you. You can put someone at ease with a few choice words. This is your gift. Though you may be an open person, you're very careful with what you say. You never want to pressure anyone because you don't like it when they do the same to you. Mercury in Aquarius pairs with Mercury in Aquarius, Taurus, Virgo, and Capricorn.

CHAPTER 12

Pisces

Pisces is the most misunderstood sign of the zodiac. There is nothing "weak" about Pisces, as many astrologers claim: He's not wishy-washy in the least. Instead, he's the pensive, strong type—instinctive and smart. In this chapter, find out more about this powerful sign.

Can You Imagine Being with Idealistic Pisces?

1. **Pisces are usually:**
   A. Inventive with brilliant minds
   B. Like secret agents: excellent at getting private information
   C. Good, loyal friends
   D. All of the above

2. **On the dark side, Pisces can sometimes be:**
   A. Overemotional
   B. Needy
   C. Controlling
   D. All of the above

3. **Pick all that apply. Pisces men have a habit of falling in love with:**
   A. Women who dominate them—who put them in their place
   B. The idea of the woman and the idea of love—not the actual woman
   C. Women from afar, whom they don't know very well
   D. Women who are much older than them

4. **A Pisces woman goes best with which male sign:**
   A. Sagittarius
   B. Taurus
   C. Gemini
   D. Libra

5. **Pisces can feel a bit more _____ than everyone else in the room.**
   A. Compassionate
   B. Beautiful
   C. Wise
   D. Cool

6. **True or false: Pisces is an Air sign.**
   A. True
   B. False

7. **How do clever Pisces people sometimes find out if a person is lying to them?**
   A. They can be sympathetic—they're very understanding, so you tell them things.
   B. They can be diplomatic—they pretend to be on your side, so you open up.
   C. They can be funny—they'll joke and get you to lower your guard.
   D. They can be nurturing—you feel safe to let them in and say the truth.

8. **If you were to take Pisces on an ideal getaway for a long weekend, where would it be?**
   A. At home—Pisces are homebodies
   B. Anywhere near the mountains and fresh air
   C. Anyplace near water—a lake, an ocean, a bay
   D. A nearby city with lots of people and things to do

9. **How may you spot a Pisces physically? They have:**
   A. Long fingers
   B. Big or kind-looking eyes
   C. A thin upper lip
   D. Wide hips for women; short and stocky for men

10. **Most Pisces men like to:**
    A. Sing
    B. Talk
    C. Offend people so that they can calm them down
    D. All of the above

Answers: 1. d, 2. c, 3. b and c, 4. a, 5. c, 6. b, 7. b, 8. c, 9. b, 10. b

The Sage

Here is the problem. It's not easy to get to the real core of Pisces. He doesn't like to wear his heart on his sleeve, and he doesn't like to share all the thoughts that go through his always-racing, complex mind. He thinks before he speaks and ponders the world—everything in it. He's also not likely to come out and say what he wants. He'll test you. His technique is to go around a subject and let you fill in the blanks. That way, he can tell if you're for him.

Personable, Clever, Intelligent

Pisces understands the world and all its different kinds of victims. In other words, a Pisces can be empathetic with any brand of misery or sadness—even if he's not sympathetic. He knows just what to say to make you feel great. He's smart all around. He can boost anyone's ego and lift anyone's spirits.

Essential

In business, he's an effective individual because he understands the heart of the matter and is able to affect the people he deals with. He's personable, intelligent, and clever. But he's never the weak soul he's portrayed to be— quite the opposite. He's as slick as a cat and just as quick.

Savvy and Sassy

Many astrologers say that Pisces is a dreamer. Not true. Instead, Pisces is a dreamer with a goal in mind. Pisces knows where she wants to be, and she tries her best to get there. She's incredibly good at her work and sometimes doesn't get the credit she deserves because she does everything without complaining—and seemingly effortlessly. Don't be fooled by tranquil Pisces. She's on top of things—always. She handles all with grace and finesse, and it's a rare occasion when things aren't handed in on time. In fact, Pisces will always go that extra mile to make a presentation just right.

The Love Package

This savvy applies to a Pisces's love life as well. Yes, Pisces wants a real love—but the package is more important than the single attributes. Each Pisces is different: Some care more about money or wealth than others, some care more about looks (though this is less of an essential factor for all Pisces), and some want a partner who will draw out their vibrant, sassy nature that lays dormant without the help of a good mate to bring it out. But one thing's for sure: Pisces wants to marry for love above all else.

The Art of Attraction

Pisces, though, can be very practical. He instinctively knows if a love match will work or if it won't. He won't stay in a relationship if he doesn't believe it's going somewhere. Also, many aspects of the relationship have to be good before he'll be convinced. If a mate is not giving, generous, and loving with him, he's not going to be those things either. However, the Pisces man differs in this regard from the Pisces woman. The Pisces woman tends to be stronger in terms of character—at least until the Pisces man comes into his own and learns from his past errors in judgment.

 **Essential**

While both Pisces men and women may worship a potential mate from afar, the Pisces woman will do something
about it. The Pisces man, on the other hand, usually keeps
quiet. He might even develop an unhealthy obsession if he
doesn't try to solve the problem and capture his heart's
desire.

The Long Haul

Pisces makes an extraordinarily good parent. There are only
two problems. Pisces could, at times, emotionally distance himself from his children when he needs to take a break from the
grind, and he is also geared to put his mate above all others . . .
including his own progeny. This is not the rule, and there can be
exceptions, of course.

Pisces does live for love—the good kind. That is, Pisces
wants real love. He wants a partner who is a lover, a best friend,
and an equal. This, too, makes Pisces an excellent choice for
a long-term mate. One thing to keep in mind, though, is that
Pisces needs a good, creative outlet in which to express himself.
Though he'll dedicate himself to a love partner and do everything in his power to make her feel nearly worshipped, he'll still
need some kind of work or hobby (even if it's just reading) that
will enable him to use his mind.

The Little Stuff Counts

While the Pisces woman is practically born refined and
sophisticated, the Pisces man can run the gamut from refined
to bohemian to trendy. Though Pisces may seem like a snob

from the outset, she is actually not so judgmental and is always diplomatic.

e✔ Fact

Actually, because Pisces is a feminine sign, the Pisces man can sometimes have effeminate qualities or, at the very least, a sympathetic ear. One physical attribute present in a Pisces man is his kind, big or catlike eyes.

The Pisces woman usually keeps up with the newest fashions, but she's never tacky. On the contrary, there's always a feminine allure to the typical Pisces woman.

What Attracts Pisces?

To attract a Pisces woman, a man must be a bit dapper but very tasteful. Loud, gaudy, or vulgar clothing (or speech) turns off a Pisces woman more quickly than you can imagine. No jewelry, please! The Pisces woman does not normally date men who wear chains or an earring. The Pisces man likes a woman with a very clean, neat look. Little or no makeup is preferred, and long hair can be a big turn-on as long as it's back, up, or simply styled. Though the Pisces man likes sexy, he'll favor a more plainly dressed—conservative, casual, or even a bit funky if it's in an artsy way—woman for the long haul.

Pillow Talk: Signs in the Bedroom

Pisces tends to be secretive about her sex life. She's not apt to relate personal details to friends or acquaintances. But one thing is for sure: When the lights go out, she turns on! Pisces is sexy, sensual, and loving. Though she's less likely than most other signs to jump from bed to bed, it's not entirely against her principles if she feels something for the person in question (even if she doesn't plan on staying forever). However, emotionless sex for a Pisces is like a fish being out of water—especially for the Pisces woman. She'll want to feel excited about you and the way things are going. That's when she'll let loose.

The Secret Pisces Man

The Pisces man, like the Pisces woman, always feels a bit above everyone else in the room. It's a smug sense of security he has, and it comes from his seemingly superior intelligence (not from self-assuredness of his looks). He may not brag, swagger, or put it out there, but the Pisces man is always convinced that one could do much worse than to be with him. In fact, he'll be quite miffed if a woman picks another man over him. He's the first to secretly list the winner's faults. He may even tell you about them. But he'll never beg. The Pisces man will never woo a woman by dropping to his knees.

Romance Counts

To seduce a Pisces man, be romantic. Open a bottle of wine, light some candles, and ask him to read you his poetry. Chances are good that he has something on hand, waiting.

 Fact

The Pisces man is passionate and sensual. He wants to be respected and appreciated for his creativity and his sharp mind. If he intuits that you're the least bit superficial or flaky, he'll run the other way.

Don't compliment him excessively on his looks—if you do, make sure to also compliment him on his personality or character: He wants a connection of the mind. Talk about the future, the world, and things of nature and beauty. Don't talk too much about your future life together. Don't push too hard too fast.

The Secret Pisces Woman

The Pisces woman is an ace at knowing just how to make the man of her choice fall head over heels in love. If she's not succeeding in doing this, she's simply with the wrong man—one who doesn't have strong feelings for her, perhaps. She has a way of operating, though, every time. Although she's nurturing and affectionate, she'll pull away to punish her man for something he's done. At this point, her mate has to make it up to her to win her back. The reason the Pisces woman does this? It works. Most men respond to her very well, indeed.

She Wants to Be Wooed and Courted

Seducing a Pisces woman is never as easy as just a good line, a handsome face, or an expensive dinner. Once again, it's the whole package. She loves to laugh and also to listen—she can be a great listener. She doesn't necessarily need to hear words of love every five minutes, but she will expect it to come out in her partner's actions when he's with her.

He must be incredibly thoughtful and treat her like a real woman. Though she tends to go for less gregarious types, she'll want an intelligent, adventurous man who will be exciting in bed, too. Earthy, exceptionally practical men turn her off and will not bring out her sultry, sensuous nature. In bed, the Pisces woman can be persuaded to try almost anything—once. She does it out of curiosity and to appease the man she loves. Yes, the Pisces woman is a gem. If she's treated like one, she won't stop at anything to treat her man like one, too.

Sun Love Matches

Pisces is a feeling sign, like all Water signs—and Fire signs as well. The whole myth "water puts out fire" is a gross misconception in the astrology world. Instead, Fire and Water are more alike than not. Fire stokes the Fire within Water, and together they balance each other out. Both are passionate, emotionally sentimental, sweet in love, and sensitive—not very likely to think or rationalize things away (like some Air or Earth signs).

The only problem in the combination of Fire and Water signs is that Fire is more independent, while Water is usually more clingy (Cancer) or possessive (Scorpio). Pisces, though, is more sensible, let's say. He doesn't usually have the typical Water traits in excess. In fact, the Pisces man can be quite independent at times. Read on to learn about the matches for the Pisces woman.

Pisces Man

This relationship can be made in heaven . . . or it just won't work. Together, the Pisces woman and the Pisces man can dream dreams, ponder the world, and intuit all things around them. Actually, they can instinctively feel each other and know what the other is thinking with astonishing accuracy. But criticism or wanting to do things "perfectly" could be an issue here. The Pisces woman holds the reins. In bed, their relationship should be sensual and erotic. If the Pisces man has some Fire in his chart, especially in his Venus or Mars, this could be a passionate, loving match. This is a very possible long-term relationship and a possible marriage, too, but the Pisces woman may be looking for a more take-charge man in her life.

Aries Man

With these two together, it seems anything is possible. Aries is the breath of fresh air the Pisces woman has been waiting for. He forces her to look at the world through optimistic eyes. He brings out her spontaneity and her femininity. He makes her feel wanted and loved—at least in the beginning. If he's really serious about winning her and keeping her, he will. If he's not, she'll sense it. Pisces is actually good for an Aries man. She encourages him with the good stuff and holds him back from going off the deep end or acting too aggressively toward others. In bed, the two are complete fireworks. Aries opens up all kinds of possibilities for Pisces, and she cherishes him for it. This can definitely be a long-term relationship, with a decent chance for marriage. However, Aries may not be able to sustain his ardor (a common theme with him).

 **Essential**

Aries, the first sign of the zodiac, is like a child. Pisces is an old soul. Together, they can balance each other out—or Pisces will get fed up and run. The Pisces woman is especially good for an Aries man. Ironically, though, is Aries good for Pisces? Only time will tell.

Taurus Man

He's stubborn. She can be stubborn. Though he inspires her and can bring out her romantic side, there always seems to be something missing in the relationship. She respects him, and he feels taken care of. He's found the nurturing, womanly soul he's been searching for. However, Pisces will not let Taurus get away with his temper tantrums, his sometimes-childish antics, his possessive moods, or his spending/being stingy binges. Taurus may be able to keep her if he's a bit more evolved than the average customer. Also, these two tend to have different senses of humor. In bed, sensual Taurus can be perfect for Pisces if there's some real affection there. Although this is not the ideal couple, it can work for a long-term relationship. These two are drawn together for sure . . . but for forever? It's a tough call.

Gemini Man

This is a difficult one. Gemini is a little self-conscious for Pisces's tastes. She wants someone a bit more direct and straightforward. Though he makes her laugh and they love to laugh at the world together, Gemini's affinity for gossiping about others can also turn the Pisces woman off. When their relationship starts, it seems as if they can move mountains—and maybe they can. But Gemini's stop-go fickle tactics will irk Pisces to no uncertain degree . . . in other words: plenty.

ⓔ✱ Essential

In truth, Pisces can be a bit refined for Gemini—and Gemini may even feel judged. But they can also seem every bit the perfect couple when they're out together.

In bed, Gemini knows exactly what to say to get Pisces going. It may even feel right, though Pisces will instinctively know they may not have a future together and this could freeze her up indefinitely. All in all, this is a possible long-term relationship, but it's not a probable marriage. Again, it depends on what the two want.

Cancer Man

It's funny how these two Water signs get along. Cancer actually confuses Pisces. She thinks she understands him, and then all of a sudden he's going off about how she's not trustworthy (or selfish). She's annoyed by this part of him. He can get possessive with her. The strange thing is, sometimes she likes it, and sometimes it makes her want to escape. No matter—Cancer is determined to woo her. In fact, he inspires her to do great things. They both love security and family, and they make wonderful parents together. Though Cancer likes kinkiness in bed more than Pisces does, he can persuade her to do almost anything he wants. If Cancer lets Pisces control things out of bed to a large degree, this can really work. It's a very possible long-term relationship and marriage.

Leo Man

Compared with Sagittarius, the Leo man is less "made for" the Pisces woman. For starters, there's always a part of the Pisces woman that Leo can't reach—and this makes him want her more. But he may get frustrated trying to dominate her, while Sagittarius and Aries will give up less easily. He wants it to be fiery, perfect love in the beginning, and this is something he wants without effort. (He's also the more sensitive of the three.)

Bed? All is fireworks and perfection. If both are willing to work at this relationship, and if Pisces doesn't get huffy with Leo when he criticizes her—making him feel guilty, which is not healthy for either of them—this can be a possible long-term relationship and maybe even a good marriage as well, depending on the match.

Fact

> Though Pisces is wonderful at making the Leo man feel every bit the powerful man he is, Leo sometimes feels that the compliments are forced (they aren't) and even, perhaps, that Pisces doesn't completely "get him."

Virgo Man

You know how they say opposites attract? Well . . . Virgo may be far too wrapped up in business pursuits to give the Pisces woman the kind of passionate relationship she dreams of. She wants romance and happily-ever-after. The Virgo man may, in fact, love and adore her, but he has trouble expressing it. Also, making love could be difficult. To Pisces, it may even feel like sexual gymnastics! He wants to change positions; she wants sensual variety. These two make good friends and even traveling partners, but marriage? A family? Probably not. If Virgo has all Fire or Water, there's a chance. If not, this is not a likely long-term relationship, and it's not a highly recommended marriage.

Libra Man

Feisty, charming Libra could seduce the Pisces woman . . . but then what? His cool reserve draws Pisces in. She wants to discover all his mysteries. However, Libra can sometimes be a bit indecisive for the Pisces woman. Though she instinctively knows how to cheer him up, she's a bit disappointed with his self-pitying ways. This match can still feel like the real thing, though—and it may just be. Pisces and Libra need time to see where the relationship is going. This is not a probable long-term relationship or marriage . . . but stranger things have happened. The harmony here is definite—but where do they go from there?

Scorpio Man

Scorpio and Pisces are like cats in heat. The lovemaking is so perfect that, when they make it out of the bedroom, they'll probably discover that they do, in fact, have much in common. Scorpio needs to open up to Pisces. Once he does, she'll feel more at ease. They can make each other laugh—in and out of bed.

 Alert

When Pisces and Scorpio get together, though, watch out! Talk about the games people play. Both are sly and clever, and they instinctively know how to get the other to do and say what they want. In fact, guilt trips abound between Scorpio and Pisces!

Though Pisces may be a bit more refined than the Scorpio man, their love for food and other sensuous pursuits go together extremely well. The only problem here is that Pisces will not let Scorpio manipulate her. He needs to feel in control, and she'll only let him feel that way if she decides to make it so. However, this can really work. They can have a probable long-term relationship and a likely (even excellent) marriage if they can get the balance right.

Sagittarius Man

Strangely enough, if there's one man put on this earth for the Pisces woman, it's the Sagittarius man. They bring out the best in one another. The Pisces woman does everything for the Archer. She makes him feel loved and protected, which is his ultimate desire with the right woman. She adores his macho, he-man ways. He excites her utterly. Pisces picks up the conversation when Sagittarius stops talking. She's a good listener. She respects Sagittarius's advice and gives him his due, and this makes him fall completely in love with her. He's also the adventurous, optimistic soul she's been searching for. This is an excellent chance for a long-term relationship . . . marriage, too: highly recommended.

Capricorn Man

What is there to say about these two except that they probably don't have much in common except their smarts? Spiritually and emotionally, they clash. Capricorn feels judged. He sees Pisces as a snob, a bit superficial and haughty for his tastes. He wants to be able to dress comfortably and casually when he feels like it. Pisces wants to spiff him up. Though he may comply, he'll resent her for it. He has a much more practical view of love, too, than idealistic Pisces. He may just burst her romantic bubble too many times. Bed, too, may be difficult—good for the short term, but the passion could fade. This is not a probable long-term relationship, and it's not a probable marriage, either. One thing is true, though: You never know with love.

Aquarius Man

Aquarius is the one sign that can really get Pisces into trouble. He inspires her to cook up mischief with him. In the beginning, they're like two peas in a pod. Pisces loves Aquarius's way of looking at the world—he fascinates her. Strangely, though, she doesn't trust him. But maybe that's because he starts letting her down. If Pisces ever does feel in love with him, she won't for long if he behaves this way. Though Pisces is sexually attracted to Aquarius, the chemistry is stronger than the love. Therefore the sex is fantastic—it just gets better and better—while the relationship dwindles. This match is confusing at times, but there's a slight possibility it could work. All in all: not a probable long-term relationship or marriage, but maybe—just maybe—if the heavens help out.

Love Planets: Venus and Mercury

Above all, remember that Pisces is the sign of the Sage. There's a born wisdom that always comes with Pisces. Pisces in anyone's chart bestows sophistication, an air of conceit, and self-assuredness. Regardless of whether it's correct—which it usually is—Pisces trusts in intuition. Pisces in your chart will always make you a bit of an idealist, or at least an optimist, depending on whether it falls in Venus or Mercury. Still, Pisces will enhance your goal-oriented nature, too. For the Pisces woman (more than the man), head-over-heels love isn't likely unless she's convinced that the person will be good for her.

Venus in Pisces

Once again, astrologers call Venus in Pisces "a dreamer, a romantic, an idealist." Along with Cancer, Pisces is one of the more starstruck of the signs—a person who lives for love. But Pisces, as opposed to other signs, wants real love—not a love. With Venus in Pisces, you want a partner to be your perfect match. That means best friend, lover, and everything to you. You also want him or her to feel the same way about you. Though you can be absolutely gaga in love, work and timing are also very important to you. Every element has to be right for you to go through with love . . . not just one component. Love must be integral and seemingly your destiny. You instinctively know the second you meet someone if you would be a good match together. Venus in Pisces goes with Venus in Libra, Scorpio, Pisces, Sagittarius, Aries, and, perhaps, Leo.

Mercury in Pisces

You go for big ideas and big visions. Nothing about you is small. You excel in communicating. Your words are refined, beautiful, and fluent, and can set the mood effortlessly. You're also wonderful at keeping the conversation going (though you don't ever talk just to fill space). You are pensive, thoughtful, and considerate. Though you don't mince words, you don't compliment just for the sake of it. You also tend to be politically diplomatic. Liars or those who shade the truth even a bit turn you off completely. Mercury in Pisces goes well with Mercury in Aries, Sagittarius, Libra, Scorpio, and Pisces.

APPENDIX A

Additional Resources

Ashman, Berne. *Sign Mates: An Astrological Guide to Love and Intimacy.* (Llewellyn Publications, 2000).

Bartlett, Sarah. *Fated Attraction: Your Complete Zodiac Guide to Seduction.* (HarperCollins, 2001).

Fenton, Sasha, and Jonathan Dee. *Moon Signs.* (Collins & Brown Limited, 2001).

Golder, Carole. *Love Lives—Using Astrology to Build the Perfect Relationship with Any Star Sign.* (Henry Holt and Company, 1990).

Holloway, Lee. *The Romantic Astrologer (A Guide to Love & Romance).* (Andrews McMeel Publishing, 2000).

Keehn, Amy. *Love and War Between the Signs.* (Prima Publishing, 1997).

Knight, Michele. *Good Sex (Starsigns).* (MQ Publications Limited, 2002).

Kosarin, Jenni. *He's Just Not in the Stars: Wicked Astrology and Uncensored Advice for Getting the (Almost) Perfect Guy.* (HarperEntertainment, 2006).

Lexander, Ren, and Geraldine Rose. *Seduction by the Stars: An Astrological Guide to Love, Lust, and Intimate Relationships.* (Bantam Doubleday Dell Publishing Group, 1995).

MacNaughton, Robin. *How to Seduce Any Man in the Zodiac.* (HarperCollins, 1995).

Petulengro, Claire. *Love Stars.* (Pan Macmillan Limited, 2003).

Pond, David. *Astrology & Relationships (Techniques for Harmonious Personal Connections).* (Llewellyn Publications, 2001).

Rathgeb, Marlene Masini. *Sexual Astrology.* (Avon Books, 1993).

West, John Anthony, and Jan Gerhard Toonder. *The Case for Astrology.* (Penguin Books, 1992).

Woolfolk, Joanna Martine. *The Only Astrology Book You'll Ever Need.* (Taylor Trade Publishing, 2011).

Quick Sun Sign Chart

Sign	Dates	Gender	Element/Quality
Aries, the Ram	3/21–4/19	M	Fire/Cardinal
Taurus, the Bull	4/20–5/20	F	Earth/Fixed
Gemini, the Twins	5/21–6/20	M	Air/Mutable
Cancer, the Crab	6/21–7/22	F	Water/Cardinal
Leo, the Lion	7/23–8/22	M	Fire/Fixed
Virgo, the Virgin	8/23–9/22	F	Earth/Mutable
Libra, the Scales	9/23–10/22	M	Air/Cardinal
Scorpio, the Scorpion	10/23–11/21	F	Water/Fixed
Sagittarius, the Archer	11/22–12/21	M	Fire/Mutable
Capricorn, the Goat	12/22–1/19	F	Earth/Cardinal
Aquarius, the Water Bearer	1/20–2/18	M	Air/Fixed
Pisces, the Fish	2/19–3/20	F	Water/Mutable

Extra: Cusp signs—that is, signs that share traits of neighboring signs—are those whose dates fall within two days of the cutoff mark. For example, someone born on February 18th or 19th is likely to have traits of Aquarius and Pisces.

Venus: Love Sign/ Mercury: Communication and Intelligence

The sign in which Venus falls describes how you are as a romantic partner or spouse, as well as what you look for in a mate. Venus also indicates how you *deal* with love, whether you're nurturing and caring, possessive or trusting, idealistic, optimistic, or otherwise.

The sign in which Mercury falls describes how you communicate your ideas. It also shows how you express yourself and how you gather and analyze information.

1950

Mercury			Venus		
Month	Day	Sign	Month	Day	Sign
JAN	1	AQU	JAN	1	AQU
JAN	15	CAP	APR	6	PIS
FEB	14	AQU	MAY	5	ARI
MAR	7	PIS	JUN	1	TAU
MAR	24	ARI	JUN	27	GEM
APR	8	TAU	JUL	22	CAN
JUN	14	GEM	AUG	16	LEO
JUL	2	CAN	SEP	10	VIR
JUL	16	LEO	OCT	4	LIB
AUG	2	VIR	OCT	28	SCO
AUG	27	LIB	NOV	21	SAG
SEP	10	VIR	DEC	14	CAP
OCT	9	LIB			
OCT	27	SCO			
NOV	15	SAG			
DEC	5	CAP			

1951

Mercury			Venus		
Month	Day	Sign	Month	Day	Sign
JAN	1	CAP	JAN	1	CAP
FEB	9	AQU	JAN	7	AQU
FEB	28	PIS	JAN	31	PIS
MAR	16	ARI	FEB	24	ARI
APR	2	TAU	MAR	21	TAU
MAY	1	ARI	APR	15	GEM
MAY	15	TAU	MAY	10	CAN
JUN	9	GEM	JUN	7	LEO
JUN	24	CAN	JUL	7	VIR
JUL	8	LEO	NOV	9	LIB
JUL	27	VIR	DEC	7	SCO
OCT	2	LIB			
OCT	19	SCO			

1951 (continued)

	Mercury		Venus
NOV	8	SAG	
DEC	1	CAP	
DEC	12	SAG	

1952

	Mercury			Venus	
Month	Day	Sign	Month	Day	Sign
JAN	1	SAG	JAN	1	SCO
JAN	13	CAP	JAN	2	SAG
FEB	3	AQU	JAN	27	CAP
FEB	20	PIS	FEB	21	AQU
MAR	7	ARI	MAR	16	PIS
MAY	14	TAU	APR	9	ARI
MAY	31	GEM	MAY	4	TAU
JUN	14	CAN	MAY	28	GEM
JUN	30	LEO	JUN	22	CAN
SEP	7	VIR	JUL	16	LEO
SEP	23	LIB	AUG	9	VIR
OCT	11	SCO	SEP	3	LIB
NOV	1	SAG	SEP	27	SCO
			OCT	22	SAG
			NOV	15	CAP
			DEC	10	AQU

1953

	Mercury			Venus	
Month	Day	Sign	Month	Day	Sign
JAN	1	SAG	JAN	1	AQU
JAN	6	CAP	JAN	5	PIS
JAN	25	AQU	FEB	2	ARI
FEB	11	PIS	MAR	14	TAU
MAR	2	ARI	MAR	31	ARI
MAR	15	PIS	JUN	5	TAU
APR	17	ARI	JUL	7	GEM

1953 (continued)

	Mercury			Venus	
MAY	8	TAU	AUG	4	CAN
MAY	23	GEM	AUG	30	LEO
JUN	6	CAN	SEP	24	VIR
JUN	26	LEO	OCT	18	LIB
JUL	28	CAN	NOV	11	SCO
AUG	11	LEO	DEC	5	SAG
AUG	30	VIR	DEC	29	CAP
SEP	15	LIB			
OCT	4	SCO			
OCT	31	SAG			
NOV	6	SCO			
DEC	10	SAG			
DEC	30	CAP			

1954

	Mercury			Venus	
Month	Day	Sign	Month	Day	Sign
JAN	1	CAP	JAN	1	CAP
JAN	18	AQU	JAN	22	AQU
FEB	4	PIS	FEB	15	PIS
APR	13	ARI	MAR	11	ARI
APR	30	TAU	APR	4	TAU
MAY	14	GEM	APR	28	GEM
MAY	30	CAN	MAY	23	CAN
AUG	7	LEO	JUN	17	LEO
AUG	22	VIR	JUL	13	VIR
SEP	8	LIB	AUG	9	LIB
SEP	29	SCO	SEP	6	SCO
NOV	4	LIB	OCT	23	SAG
NOV	11	SCO	OCT	27	SCO
DEC	4	SAG			
DEC	23	CAP			

1955

Mercury			Venus		
Month	Day	Sign	Month	Day	Sign
JAN	1	CAP	JAN	1	SCO
JAN	10	AQU	JAN	6	SAG
MAR	17	PIS	FEB	6	CAP
APR	6	ARI	MAR	4	AQU
APR	22	TAU	MAR	30	PIS
MAY	6	GEM	APR	24	ARI
JUL	13	CAN	MAY	19	TAU
JUL	30	LEO	JUN	13	GEM
AUG	14	VIR	JUL	8	CAN
SEP	1	LIB	AUG	1	LEO
NOV	8	SCO	AUG	25	VIR
NOV	27	SAG	SEP	18	LIB
DEC	16	CAP	OCT	13	SCO
			NOV	6	SAG
			NOV	30	CAP
			DEC	24	AQU

1956

Mercury			Venus		
Month	Day	Sign	Month	Day	Sign
JAN	1	CAP	JAN	1	AQU
JAN	4	AQU	JAN	17	PIS
FEB	2	CAP	FEB	11	ARI
FEB	15	AQU	MAR	7	TAU
MAR	11	PIS	APR	4	GEM
MAR	28	ARI	MAY	8	CAN
APR	12	TAU	JUN	23	GEM
APR	29	GEM	AUG	4	CAN
JUL	6	CAN	SEP	8	LEO
JUL	21	LEO	OCT	6	VIR
AUG	5	VIR	OCT	31	LIB
AUG	26	LIB	NOV	25	SCO
SEP	29	VIR	DEC	19	SAG

1956 (continued)

	Mercury		Venus
OCT	11	LIB	
OCT	31	SCO	
NOV	18	SAG	
DEC	8	CAP	

1957

	Mercury			Venus	
Month	Day	Sign	Month	Day	Sign
JAN	1	CAP	JAN	1	SAG
FEB	12	AQU	JAN	12	CAP
MAR	4	PIS	FEB	5	AQU
MAR	20	ARI	MAR	1	PIS
APR	4	TAU	MAR	25	ARI
JUN	12	GEM	APR	19	TAU
JUN	28	CAN	MAY	13	GEM
JUL	12	LEO	JUN	6	CAN
JUL	30	VIR	JUL	1	LEO
OCT	6	LIB	JUL	26	VIR
OCT	23	SCO	AUG	20	LIB
NOV	11	SAG	SEP	14	SCO
DEC	2	CAP	OCT	10	SAG
DEC	28	SAG	NOV	5	CAP
			DEC	6	AQU

1958

	Mercury			Venus	
Month	Day	Sign	Month	Day	Sign
JAN	1	SAG	JAN	1	AQU
JAN	14	CAP	APR	6	PIS
FEB	6	AQU	MAY	5	ARI
FEB	24	PIS	JUN	1	TAU
MAR	12	ARI	JUN	26	GEM
APR	2	TAU	JUL	22	CAN
APR	10	ARI	AUG	16	LEO

1958 (continued)

	Mercury			Venus	
MAY	17	TAU	SEP	9	VIR
JUN	5	GEM	OCT	3	LIB
JUN	20	CAN	OCT	27	SCO
JUL	4	LEO	NOV	20	SAG
JUL	26	VIR	DEC	14	CAP
AUG	23	LEO			
SEP	11	VIR			
SEP	28	LIB			
OCT	16	SCO			
NOV	5	SAG			

1959

	Mercury			Venus	
Month	Day	Sign	Month	Day	Sign
JAN	1	SAG	JAN	1	CAP
JAN	10	CAP	JAN	7	AQU
JAN	30	AQU	JAN	31	PIS
FEB	17	PIS	FEB	24	ARI
MAR	5	ARI	MAR	20	TAU
MAY	12	TAU	APR	14	GEM
MAY	28	GEM	MAY	10	CAN
JUN	11	CAN	JUN	6	LEO
JUN	28	LEO	JUL	8	VIR
SEP	5	VIR	SEP	20	LEO
OCT	21	LIB	SEP	25	VIR
OCT	9	SCO	NOV	9	LIB
OCT	31	SAG	DEC	7	SCO
NOV	25	SCO			
DEC	13	SAG			

1960

	Mercury			Venus	
Month	Day	Sign	Month	Day	Sign
JAN	1	SAG	JAN	1	SCO
JAN	4	CAP	JAN	2	SAG
JAN	23	AQU	JAN	27	CAP
FEB	9	PIS	FEB	20	AQU
APR	16	ARI	MAR	16	PIS
MAY	4	TAU	APR	9	ARI
MAY	19	GEM	MAY	3	TAU
JUN	2	CAN	MAY	28	GEM
JUL	1	LEO	JUN	21	CAN
JUL	6	CAN	JUL	16	LEO
AUG	10	LEO	AUG	9	VIR
AUG	27	VIR	SEP	2	LIB
SEP	12	LIB	SEP	27	SCO
OCT	1	SCO	OCT	21	SAG
DEC	7	SAG	NOV	15	CAP
DEC	27	CAP	DEC	10	AQU

1961

	Mercury			Venus	
Month	Day	Sign	Month	Day	Sign
JAN	1	CAP	JAN	1	AQU
JAN	14	AQU	JAN	5	PIS
FEB	1	PIS	FEB	2	ARI
FEB	24	AQU	JUN	5	TAU
MAR	18	PIS	JUL	7	GEM
APR	10	ARI	AUG	3	CAN
APR	26	TAU	AUG	29	LEO
MAY	10	GEM	SEP	23	VIR
MAY	28	CAN	OCT	18	LIB
AUG	4	LEO	NOV	11	SCO
AUG	18	VIR	DEC	5	SAG
SEP	4	LIB	DEC	29	CAP
SEP	27	SCO			

1961 (continued)

	Mercury		Venus
OCT	22	LIB	
NOV	10	SCO	
NOV	30	SAG	
DEC	20	CAP	

1962

Mercury			Venus		
Month	Day	Sign	Month	Day	Sign
JAN	1	CAP	JAN	1	CAP
JAN	7	AQU	JAN	21	AQU
MAR	15	PIS	FEB	14	PIS
APR	3	ARI	MAR	10	ARI
APR	18	TAU	APR	3	TAU
MAY	3	GEM	APR	28	GEM
JUL	11	CAN	MAY	23	CAN
JUL	26	LEO	JUN	17	LEO
AUG	10	VIR	JUL	12	VIR
AUG	29	LIB	AUG	8	LIB
NOV	5	SCO	SEP	7	SCO
NOV	23	SAG			
DEC	12	CAP			

1963

Mercury			Venus		
Month	Day	Sign	Month	Day	Sign
JAN	1	CAP	JAN	1	SCO
JAN	2	AQU	JAN	6	SAG
JAN	20	CAP	FEB	5	CAP
FEB	15	AQU	MAR	4	AQU
MAR	9	PIS	MAR	30	PIS
MAR	26	ARI	APR	24	ARI
APR	9	TAU	MAY	19	TAU
MAY	3	GEM	JUN	12	GEM
MAY	10	TAU	JUL	7	CAN

1963 (continued)

	Mercury			Venus	
JUN	14	GEM	JUL	31	LEO
JUL	4	CAN	AUG	25	VIR
JUL	18	LEO	SEP	18	LIB
AUG	3	VIR	OCT	12	SCO
AUG	26	LIB	NOV	5	SAG
SEP	16	VIR	NOV	29	CAP
OCT	10	LIB	DEC	23	AQU
OCT	28	SCO			
NOV	16	SAG			
DEC	6	CAP			

1964

	Mercury			Venus	
Month	Day	Sign	Month	Day	Sign
JAN	1	CAP	JAN	1	AQU
FEB	10	AQU	JAN	17	PIS
FEB	29	PIS	FEB	10	ARI
MAR	16	ARI	MAR	7	TAU
APR	2	TAU	APR	4	GEM
JUN	9	GEM	MAY	9	CAN
JUN	24	CAN	JUN	17	GEM
JUL	9	LEO	AUG	5	CAN
JUL	27	VIR	SEP	8	LEO
OCT	3	LIB	OCT	5	VIR
OCT	20	SCO	OCT	31	LIB
NOV	8	SAG	NOV	25	SCO
NOV	30	CAP	DEC	19	SAG
DEC	16	SAG			

1965

	Mercury			Venus	
Month	Day	Sign	Month	Day	Sign
JAN	1	SAG	JAN	1	SAG
JAN	13	CAP	JAN	12	CAP

1965 (continued)

	Mercury			Venus	
FEB	3	AQU	FEB	5	AQU
FEB	21	PIS	MAR	1	PIS
MAR	9	ARI	MAR	25	ARI
MAY	15	TAU	APR	18	TAU
JUN	2	GEM	MAY	12	GEM
JUN	16	CAN	JUN	6	CAN
JUL	1	LEO	JUN	30	LEO
JUL	31	VIR	JUL	25	VIR
AUG	3	LEO	AUG	19	LIB
SEP	8	VIR	SEP	13	SCO
SEP	25	LIB	OCT	9	SAG
OCT	12	SCO	NOV	5	CAP
NOV	2	SAG	DEC	7	AQU

1966

	Mercury			Venus	
Month	Day	Sign	Month	Day	Sign
JAN	1	SAG	JAN	1	AQU
JAN	7	CAP	FEB	6	CAP
JAN	27	AQU	FEB	25	AQU
FEB	13	PIS	APR	6	PIS
MAR	3	ARI	MAY	5	ARI
MAR	22	PIS	MAY	31	TAU
APR	17	ARI	JUN	26	GEM
MAY	9	TAU	JUL	21	CAN
MAY	24	GEM	AUG	15	LEO
JUN	7	CAN	SEP	8	VIR
JUN	26	LEO	OCT	3	LIB
SEP	1	VIR	OCT	27	SCO
SEP	17	LIB	NOV	20	SAG
OCT	5	SCO	DEC	13	CAP
OCT	30	SAG			
NOV	13	SCO			
DEC	11	SAG			

1967

	Mercury			Venus	
Month	Day	Sign	Month	Day	Sign
JAN	1	CAP	JAN	1	CAP
JAN	19	AQU	JAN	6	AQU
FEB	6	PIS	JAN	30	PIS
APR	14	ARI	FEB	23	ARI
MAY	1	TAU	MAR	20	TAU
MAY	16	GEM	APR	14	GEM
MAY	31	CAN	MAY	10	CAN
AUG	8	LEO	JUN	6	LEO
AUG	24	VIR	JUL	8	VIR
SEP	9	LIB	SEP	9	LEO
SEP	30	SCO	OCT	1	VIR
DEC	5	SAG	NOV	9	LIB
DEC	24	CAP	DEC	7	SCO

1968

	Mercury			Venus	
Month	Day	Sign	Month	Day	Sign
JAN	1	CAP	JAN	1	SAG
JAN	12	AQU	JAN	26	CAP
FEB	1	PIS	FEB	20	AQU
FEB	11	AQU	MAR	15	PIS
MAR	17	PIS	APR	8	ARI
APR	7	ARI	MAY	3	TAU
APR	22	TAU	MAY	27	GEM
MAY	6	GEM	JUN	21	CAN
MAY	29	CAN	JUL	15	LEO
JUN	13	GEM	AUG	8	VIR
JUL	13	CAN	SEP	2	LIB
JUL	31	LEO	SEP	26	SCO
AUG	15	VIR	OCT	21	SAG
SEP	1	LIB	NOV	14	CAP
SEP	28	SCO	DEC	9	AQU
OCT	7	LIB			

1968 (continued)

	Mercury		Venus
NOV	8	SCO	
NOV	27	SAG	
DEC	16	CAP	

1969

	Mercury			Venus	
Month	Day	Sign	Month	Day	Sign
JAN	1	CAP	JAN	1	AQU
JAN	4	AQU	JAN	4	PIS
MAR	12	PIS	FEB	2	ARI
MAR	30	ARI	JUN	6	TAU
APR	14	TAU	JUL	6	GEM
APR	30	GEM	AUG	3	CAN
JUL	8	CAN	AUG	29	LEO
JUL	22	LEO	SEP	23	VIR
AUG	7	VIR	OCT	17	LIB
AUG	27	LIB	NOV	10	SCO
OCT	7	VIR	DEC	4	SAG
OCT	9	LIB	DEC	28	CAP
NOV	1	SCO			
NOV	20	SAG			
DEC	9	CAP			

1970

	Mercury			Venus	
Month	Day	Sign	Month	Day	Sign
JAN	1	CAP	JAN	1	CAP
JAN	4	AQU	JAN	21	AQU
JAN	4	CAP	FEB	14	PIS
FEB	13	AQU	MAR	10	ARI
MAR	5	PIS	APR	3	TAU
MAR	22	ARI	APR	27	GEM
APR	6	TAU	MAY	22	CAN
JUN	13	GEM	JUN	16	LEO

1970 (continued)

	Mercury			Venus	
JUN	30	CAN	JUL	12	VIR
JUL	14	LEO	AUG	8	LIB
JUL	31	VIR	SEP	7	SCO
OCT	7	LIB			
OCT	25	SCO			
NOV	13	SAG			
DEC	3	CAP			

1971

	Mercury			Venus	
Month	Day	Sign	Month	Day	Sign
JAN	1	CAP	JAN	1	SCO
JAN	2	SAG	JAN	7	SAG
JAN	14	CAP	FEB	5	CAP
FEB	7	AQU	MAR	4	AQU
FEB	26	PIS	MAR	29	PIS
MAR	14	ARI	APR	23	ARI
APR	1	TAU	MAY	18	TAU
APR	18	ARI	JUN	12	GEM
MAY	17	TAU	JUL	6	CAN
JUN	7	GEM	JUL	31	LEO
JUN	21	CAN	AUG	24	VIR
JUL	6	LEO	SEP	17	LIB
JUL	26	VIR	OCT	11	SCO
AUG	29	LEO	NOV	5	SAG
SEP	11	VIR	NOV	29	CAP
SEP	30	LIB	DEC	23	AQU
OCT	17	SCO			
NOV	6	SAG			

1972

	Mercury			Venus	
Month	Day	Sign	Month	Day	Sign
JAN	1	SAG	JAN	1	AQU
JAN	11	CAP	JAN	16	PIS
JAN	31	AQU	FEB	10	ARI
FEB	18	PIS	MAR	7	TAU
MAR	5	ARI	APR	3	GEM
MAY	12	TAU	MAY	10	CAN
MAY	29	GEM	JUN	11	GEM
JUN	12	CAN	AUG	6	CAN
JUN	28	LEO	SEP	7	LEO
SEP	5	VIR	OCT	5	VIR
SEP	21	LIB	OCT	30	LIB
OCT	9	SCO	NOV	24	SCO
OCT	30	SAG	DEC	18	SAG
NOV	29	SCO			
DEC	12	SAG			

1973

	Mercury			Venus	
Month	Day	Sign	Month	Day	Sign
JAN	1	SAG	JAN	1	SAG
JAN	4	CAP	JAN	11	CAP
JAN	23	AQU	FEB	4	AQU
FEB	9	PIS	FEB	28	PIS
APR	16	ARI	MAR	24	ARI
MAY	6	TAU	APR	18	TAU
MAY	20	GEM	MAY	12	GEM
JUN	4	CAN	JUN	5	CAN
JUN	27	LEO	JUN	30	LEO
JUL	16	CAN	JUL	25	VIR
AUG	11	LEO	AUG	19	LIB
AUG	28	VIR	SEP	13	SCO
SEP	13	LIB	OCT	9	SAG

1973 (continued)

	Mercury			Venus	
OCT	2	SCO	NOV	5	CAP
DEC	8	SAG	DEC	7	AQU
DEC	28	CAP			

1974

	Mercury			Venus	
Month	Day	Sign	Month	Day	Sign
JAN	1	CAP	JAN	1	AQU
JAN	16	AQU	JAN	29	CAP
FEB	2	PIS	FEB	28	AQU
MAR	2	AQU	APR	6	PIS
MAR	17	PIS	MAY	4	ARI
APR	11	ARI	MAY	31	TAU
APR	28	TAU	JUN	25	GEM
MAY	12	GEM	JUL	21	CAN
MAY	29	CAN	AUG	14	LEO
AUG	5	LEO	SEP	8	VIR
AUG	20	VIR	OCT	2	LIB
SEP	6	LIB	OCT	26	SCO
SEP	28	SCO	NOV	19	SAG
OCT	26	LIB	DEC	13	CAP
NOV	11	SCO			
DEC	2	SAG			
DEC	21	CAP			

1975

	Mercury			Venus	
Month	Day	Sign	Month	Day	Sign
JAN	1	CAP	JAN	1	CAP
JAN	8	AQU	JAN	6	AQU
MAR	16	PIS	JAN	30	PIS
APR	4	ARI	FEB	23	ARI
APR	19	TAU	MAR	19	TAU

1975 (continued)

	Mercury			Venus	
MAY	4	GEM	APR	13	GEM
JUL	12	CAN	MAY	9	CAN
JUL	28	LEO	JUN	6	LEO
AUG	12	VIR	JUL	9	VIR
AUG	30	LIB	SEP	2	LEO
NOV	6	SCO	OCT	4	VIR
NOV	25	SAG	NOV	9	LIB
DEC	14	CAP	DEC	7	SCO

1976

	Mercury			Venus	
Month	Day	Sign	Month	Day	Sign
JAN	1	CAP	JAN	1	SAG
JAN	2	AQU	JAN	26	CAP
JAN	25	CAP	FEB	19	AQU
FEB	15	AQU	MAR	15	PIS
MAR	9	PIS	APR	8	ARI
MAR	26	ARI	MAY	2	TAU
APR	10	TAU	MAY	27	GEM
APR	29	GEM	JUN	20	CAN
MAY	19	TAU	JUL	14	LEO
JUN	13	GEM	AUG	8	VIR
JUL	4	CAN	SEP	1	LIB
JUL	18	LEO	SEP	26	SCO
AUG	3	VIR	OCT	20	SAG
AUG	25	LIB	NOV	14	CAP
SEP	21	VIR	DEC	9	AQU
OCT	10	LIB			
OCT	29	SCO			
NOV	16	SAG			
DEC	6	CAP			

1977

	Mercury			Venus	
Month	Day	Sign	Month	Day	Sign
JAN	1	CAP	JAN	1	AQU
FEB	10	AQU	JAN	4	PIS
MAR	2	PIS	FEB	2	ARI
MAR	18	ARI	JUN	6	TAU
APR	3	TAU	JUL	6	GEM
JUN	10	GEM	AUG	2	CAN
JUN	26	CAN	AUG	28	LEO
JUL	10	LEO	SEP	22	VIR
JUL	28	VIR	OCT	17	LIB
OCT	4	LIB	NOV	10	SCO
OCT	21	SCO	DEC	4	SAG
NOV	9	SAG	DEC	27	CAP
DEC	1	CAP			
DEC	21	SAG			

1978

	Mercury			Venus	
Month	Day	Sign	Month	Day	Sign
JAN	1	SAG	JAN	1	CAP
JAN	13	CAP	JAN	20	AQU
FEB	4	AQU	FEB	13	PIS
FEB	22	PIS	MAR	9	ARI
MAR	10	ARI	APR	2	TAU
MAY	16	TAU	APR	27	GEM
JUN	3	GEM	MAY	22	CAN
JUN	17	CAN	JUN	16	LEO
JUL	2	LEO	JUL	12	VIR
JUL	27	VIR	AUG	8	LIB
AUG	13	LEO	SEP	7	SCO
SEP	9	VIR			
SEP	26	LIB			
OCT	14	SCO			
NOV	3	SAG			

1979

	Mercury			Venus	
Month	Day	Sign	Month	Day	Sign
JAN	1	SAG	JAN	1	SCO
JAN	8	CAP	JAN	7	SAG
JAN	28	AQU	FEB	5	CAP
FEB	14	PIS	MAR	3	AQU
MAR	3	ARI	MAR	29	PIS
MAR	28	PIS	APR	23	ARI
APR	17	ARI	MAY	18	TAU
MAY	10	TAU	JUN	11	GEM
MAY	26	GEM	JUL	6	CAN
JUN	9	CAN	JUL	30	LEO
JUN	27	LEO	AUG	24	VIR
SEP	2	VIR	SEP	17	LIB
SEP	18	LIB	OCT	11	SCO
OCT	7	SCO	NOV	4	SAG
OCT	30	SAG	NOV	28	CAP
NOV	18	SCO	DEC	22	AQU
DEC	12	SAG			

1980

	Mercury			Venus	
Month	Day	Sign	Month	Day	Sign
JAN	1	SAG	JAN	1	AQU
JAN	2	CAP	JAN	16	PIS
JAN	21	AQU	FEB	9	ARI
FEB	7	PIS	MAR	6	TAU
APR	14	ARI	APR	3	GEM
MAY	2	TAU	MAY	12	CAN
MAY	16	GEM	JUN	5	GEM
MAY	31	CAN	AUG	6	CAN
AUG	9	LEO	SEP	7	LEO
AUG	24	VIR	OCT	4	VIR
SEP	10	LIB	OCT	30	LIB
SEP	30	SCO	NOV	24	SCO

1980 (continued)

	Mercury			Venus	
DEC	5	SAG	DEC	18	SAG
DEC	25	CAP			

1981

	Mercury			Venus	
Month	Day	Sign	Month	Day	Sign
JAN	1	CAP	JAN	1	SAG
JAN	12	AQU	JAN	11	CAP
JAN	31	PIS	FEB	4	AQU
FEB	16	AQU	FEB	28	PIS
MAR	18	PIS	MAR	24	ARI
APR	8	ARI	APR	17	TAU
APR	24	TAU	MAY	11	GEM
MAY	8	GEM	JUN	5	CAN
MAY	28	CAN	JUN	29	LEO
JUN	22	GEM	JUL	24	VIR
JUL	12	CAN	AUG	18	LIB
AUG	1	LEO	SEP	12	SCO
AUG	16	VIR	OCT	9	SAG
SEP	2	LIB	NOV	5	CAP
SEP	27	SCO	DEC	8	AQU
OCT	14	LIB			
NOV	9	SCO			
NOV	28	SAG			
DEC	17	CAP			

1982

	Mercury			Venus	
Month	Day	Sign	Month	Day	Sign
JAN	1	CAP	JAN	1	AQU
JAN	5	AQU	JAN	23	CAP
MAR	13	PIS	MAR	2	AQU
MAR	31	ARI	APR	6	PIS

1982 (continued)

	Mercury			Venus	
APR	15	TAU	MAY	4	ARI
MAY	1	GEM	MAY	30	TAU
JUL	9	CAN	JUN	25	GEM
JUL	24	LEO	JUL	20	CAN
AUG	8	VIR	AUG	14	LEO
AUG	28	LIB	SEP	7	VIR
NOV	3	SCO	OCT	2	LIB
NOV	21	SAG	OCT	26	SCO
DEC	10	CAP	NOV	18	SAG
			DEC	12	CAP

1983

	Mercury			Venus	
Month	Day	Sign	Month	Day	Sign
JAN	1	AQU	JAN	1	CAP
JAN	12	CAP	JAN	5	AQU
FEB	14	AQU	JAN	29	PIS
MAR	7	PIS	FEB	22	ARI
MAR	23	ARI	MAR	19	TAU
APR	7	TAU	APR	13	GEM
JUN	14	GEM	MAY	9	CAN
JUL	1	CAN	JUN	6	LEO
JUL	15	LEO	JUL	10	VIR
AUG	1	VIR	AUG	27	LEO
AUG	29	LIB	OCT	5	VIR
SEP	6	VIR	NOV	9	LIB
OCT	8	LIB	DEC	6	SCO
OCT	26	SCO			
NOV	14	SAG			
DEC	4	CAP			

1984

	Mercury			Venus	
Month	Day	Sign	Month	Day	Sign
JAN	1	CAP	JAN	1	SAG
FEB	9	AQU	JAN	25	CAP
FEB	27	PIS	FEB	19	AQU
MAR	14	ARI	MAR	14	PIS
MAR	31	TAU	APR	7	ARI
APR	25	ARI	MAY	2	TAU
MAY	15	TAU	MAY	26	GEM
JUN	7	GEM	JUN	20	CAN
JUN	22	CAN	JUL	14	LEO
JUL	6	LEO	AUG	7	VIR
JUL	26	VIR	SEP	1	LIB
SEP	30	LIB	SEP	25	SCO
OCT	18	SCO	OCT	20	SAG
NOV	6	SAG	NOV	13	CAP
DEC	1	CAP	DEC	9	AQU
DEC	7	SAG			

1985

	Mercury			Venus	
Month	Day	Sign	Month	Day	Sign
JAN	1	SAG	JAN	1	AQU
JAN	11	CAP	JAN	4	PIS
FEB	1	AQU	FEB	2	ARI
FEB	18	PIS	JUN	6	TAU
MAR	7	ARI	JUL	6	GEM
MAY	14	TAU	AUG	2	CAN
MAY	30	GEM	AUG	28	LEO
JUN	13	CAN	SEP	22	VIR
JUN	29	LEO	OCT	16	LIB
SEP	6	VIR	NOV	9	SCO
SEP	22	LIB	DEC	3	SAG
OCT	10	SCO	DEC	27	CAP
OCT	31	SAG			

1985 (continued)

	Mercury		Venus
DEC	4	SCO	
DEC	12	SAG	

1986

	Mercury			Venus	
Month	Day	Sign	Month	Day	Sign
JAN	1	SAG	JAN	1	CAP
JAN	5	CAP	JAN	20	AQU
JAN	25	AQU	FEB	13	PIS
FEB	11	PIS	MAR	9	ARI
MAR	3	ARI	APR	2	TAU
MAR	11	PIS	APR	26	GEM
APR	17	ARI	MAY	21	CAN
MAY	7	TAU	JUN	15	LEO
MAY	22	GEM	JUL	11	VIR
JUN	5	CAN	AUG	7	LIB
JUN	26	LEO	SEP	7	SCO
JUL	23	CAN			
AUG	11	LEO			
AUG	30	VIR			
SEP	15	LIB			
OCT	4	SCO			
DEC	10	SAG			
DEC	29	CAP			

1987

	Mercury			Venus	
Month	Day	Sign	Month	Day	Sign
JAN	1	CAP	JAN	1	SCO
JAN	17	AQU	JAN	7	SAG
FEB	4	PIS	FEB	5	CAP
MAR	11	AQU	MAR	3	AQU
MAR	13	PIS	MAR	28	PIS
APR	12	ARI	APR	22	ARI

1987 (continued)

	Mercury			Venus	
APR	29	TAU	MAY	17	TAU
MAY	13	GEM	JUN	11	GEM
MAY	30	CAN	JUL	5	CAN
AUG	6	LEO	JUL	30	LEO
AUG	21	VIR	AUG	23	VIR
SEP	7	LIB	SEP	16	LIB
SEP	28	SCO	OCT	10	SCO
NOV	1	LIB	NOV	3	SAG
NOV	11	SCO	NOV	28	CAP
DEC	3	SAG	DEC	22	AQU
DEC	22	CAP			

1988

	Mercury			Venus	
Month	Day	Sign	Month	Day	Sign
JAN	1	CAP	JAN	1	AQU
JAN	10	AQU	JAN	15	PIS
MAR	16	PIS	FEB	9	ARI
APR	4	ARI	MAR	6	TAU
APR	20	TAU	APR	3	GEM
MAY	4	GEM	MAY	17	CAN
JUL	12	CAN	MAY	27	GEM
JUL	28	LEO	AUG	6	CAN
AUG	12	VIR	SEP	7	LEO
AUG	30	LIB	OCT	4	VIR
NOV	6	SCO	OCT	29	LIB
NOV	25	SAG	NOV	23	SCO
DEC	14	CAP	DEC	17	SAG

1989

	Mercury			Venus	
Month	Day	Sign	Month	Day	Sign
JAN	1	CAP	JAN	1	SAG
JAN	3	AQU	JAN	10	CAP

1989 (continued)

Mercury			Venus		
JAN	30	CAP	FEB	3	AQU
FEB	15	AQU	FEB	27	PIS
MAR	11	PIS	MAR	23	ARI
MAR	29	ARI	APR	16	TAU
APR	11	TAU	MAY	11	GEM
APR	29	GEM	JUN	4	CAN
MAY	28	TAU	JUN	29	LEO
JUN	12	GEM	JUL	24	VIR
JUL	6	CAN	AUG	18	LIB
JUL	20	LEO	SEP	12	SCO
AUG	5	VIR	OCT	8	SAG
AUG	26	LIB	NOV	5	CAP
SEP	26	VIR	DEC	10	AQU
OCT	11	LIB			
OCT	30	SCO			
NOV	18	SAG			
DEC	7	CAP			

1990

Mercury			Venus		
Month	Day	Sign	Month	Day	Sign
JAN	1	CAP	JAN	1	AQU
FEB	12	AQU	JAN	16	CAP
MAR	3	PIS	MAR	3	AQU
MAR	20	ARI	APR	6	PIS
APR	4	TAU	MAY	4	ARI
JUN	12	GEM	MAY	30	TAU
JUN	27	CAN	JUN	25	GEM
JUL	11	LEO	JUL	20	CAN
JUL	29	VIR	AUG	13	LEO
OCT	5	LIB	SEP	7	VIR
OCT	23	SCO	OCT	1	LIB
NOV	11	SAG	OCT	25	SCO
DEC	2	CAP	NOV	18	SAG
DEC	25	SAG	DEC	12	CAP

1991

Month	Day	Sign	Month	Day	Sign
	Mercury			Venus	
JAN	1	SAG	JAN	1	CAP
JAN	15	CAP	JAN	5	AQU
FEB	6	AQU	JAN	28	PIS
FEB	20	PIS	FEB	22	ARI
MAR	12	ARI	MAR	18	TAU
MAY	17	TAU	APR	12	GEM
JUN	6	GEM	MAY	8	CAN
JUN	20	CAN	JUN	5	LEO
JUL	5	LEO	JUL	11	VIR
JUL	27	VIR	AUG	21	LEO
AUG	20	LEO	OCT	6	VIR
SEP	11	VIR	NOV	9	LIB
SEP	29	LIB	DEC	6	SCO
OCT	16	SCO	DEC	31	SAG
NOV	5	SAG			

1992

Month	Day	Sign	Month	Day	Sign
	Mercury			Venus	
JAN	1	SAG	JAN	1	SAG
JAN	11	CAP	JAN	25	CAP
JAN	30	AQU	FEB	18	AQU
FEB	17	PIS	MAR	13	PIS
MAR	4	ARI	APR	7	ARI
APR	4	PIS	MAY	1	TAU
APR	15	ARI	MAY	25	GEM
MAY	12	TAU	JUN	19	CAN
MAY	27	GEM	JUL	13	LEO
JUN	10	CAN	AUG	7	VIR
JUN	28	LEO	AUG	31	LIB
SEP	4	VIR	SEP	24	SCO
SEP	20	LIB	OCT	19	SAG
OCT	8	SCO	NOV	13	CAP

1992 (continued)

	Mercury			Venus	
OCT	30	SAG	DEC	8	AQU
NOV	22	SCO			
DEC	13	SAG			

1993

Mercury			Venus		
Month	Day	Sign	Month	Day	Sign
JAN	1	SAG	JAN	1	AQU
JAN	3	CAP	JAN	3	PIS
JAN	22	AQU	FEB	2	ARI
FEB	8	PIS	JUN	6	TAU
APR	16	ARI	JUL	5	GEM
MAY	4	TAU	AUG	1	CAN
MAY	19	GEM	AUG	27	LEO
JUN	3	CAN	SEP	21	VIR
AUG	11	LEO	OCT	15	LIB
AUG	27	VIR	NOV	8	SCO
SEP	12	LIB	DEC	2	SAG
OCT	2	SCO	DEC	26	CAP
DEC	8	SAG			
DEC	27	CAP			

1994

Mercury			Venus		
Month	Day	Sign	Month	Day	Sign
JAN	1	CAP	JAN	1	CAP
JAN	15	AQU	JAN	19	AQU
FEB	2	PIS	FEB	12	PIS
FEB	22	AQU	MAR	8	ARI
MAR	19	PIS	APR	1	TAU
APR	10	ARI	APR	26	GEM
APR	26	TAU	MAY	20	CAN
MAY	10	GEM	JUN	15	LEO
MAY	29	CAN	JUL	11	VIR

1994 (continued)

	Mercury			Venus	
JUL	3	GEM	AUG	7	LIB
JUL	11	CAN	SEP	7	SCO
AUG	4	LEO			
AUG	19	VIR			
SEP	5	LIB			
SEP	28	SCO			
OCT	20	LIB			
NOV	11	SCO			
DEC	1	SAG			
DEC	21	CAP			

1995

	Mercury			Venus	
Month	Day	Sign	Month	Day	Sign
JAN	1	CAP	JAN	1	SAG
JAN	7	AQU	JAN	7	SAG
MAR	15	PIS	FEB	4	CAP
APR	3	ARI	MAR	2	AQU
APR	18	TAU	MAR	28	PIS
MAY	3	GEM	APR	21	ARI
JUL	11	CAN	MAY	16	TAU
JUL	26	LEO	JUN	10	GEM
AUG	11	VIR	JUL	5	CAN
AUG	30	LIB	JUL	29	LEO
NOV	5	SCO	AUG	22	VIR
NOV	23	SAG	SEP	16	LIB
DEC	14	CAP	OCT	10	SCO
			NOV	3	SAG
			NOV	27	CAP
			DEC	21	AQU

Index

L

Z

We Have

EVERYTHING

on Anything!

The Everything® list spans a wide range of subjects, with more than 500 titles covering 25 different categories:

Business	History	Reference
Careers	Home Improvement	Religion
Children's Storybooks	Everything Kids	Self-Help
Computers	Languages	Sports & Fitness
Cooking	Music	Travel
Crafts and Hobbies	New Age	Wedding
Education/Schools	Parenting	Writing
Games and Puzzles	Personal Finance	
Health	Pets	